Women and Leadership

Florence L. Denmark · Michele A. Paludi
Editors

Women and Leadership

Springer

Editors
Florence L. Denmark
Department of Psychology
Pace University
New York, NY, USA

Michele A. Paludi
Excelsior College
Albany, NY, USA

ISBN 978-3-030-10164-0 ISBN 978-3-319-72182-8 (eBook)
https://doi.org/10.1007/978-3-319-72182-8

Printed on acid-free paper

This Springer imprint is published by the registered company Springer International Publishing AG part of Springer Nature.
The registered company address is: Gewerbestrasse 11, 6330 Cham, Switzerland

Whether there are innately female leadership styles…is not really the right question. It is more important to ask why there has been so little attention paid to women leaders over the years as well as why the styles of leading more often exhibited by women are particularly useful at this critical moment in history.

Charlotte Bunch

We dedicate this book to girls who strive to become leaders.

Preface

No country can ever truly flourish if it stifles the potential of its women and deprives itself of the contributions of half of its citizens.

Michelle Obama

You have to look at leadership through the eyes of the followers and you have to live the message. What I have learned is that people become motivated when you guide them to the source of their own power and when you make heroes out of employees who personify what you want to see in the organization.

Anita Roddick

Leadership is not about a title or a designation. It's about impact, influence and inspiration. Impact involves getting results, influence is about spreading the passion you have for your work, and you have to inspire team-mates and customers.

Robin S. Sharma

In 1982, Ann Hopkins, a senior manager in Price Waterhouse's Office of Government Services, was being considered for Partnership in the firm. She was 1 of 88 candidates for this position and was the sole woman candidate. She received high praise from other partners, yet her candidacy was put on indefinite hold. Ms. Hopkins eventually resigned and sued Price Waterhouse for sex discrimination, in which she argued that her lack of promotion followed pressure for her to walk, dress, talk, and act more "femininely" (Levit, 1998). Her case reached the United States Supreme Court, which ruled 6–3 that Price Waterhouse discriminated against Ms. Hopkins based on sex stereotypes. As Justice Brennan wrote: "An employer who objects to aggressiveness in women but whose positions require this trait places women in an intolerable and impermissible Catch-22: out of a job if they behave aggressively and out of a job if they don't" (*Price Waterhouse v. Hopkins, 490*).

Swartz (2017) noted that women leaders have faced obstacles during three periods in modern history:

1. The Concrete Wall of the pre-1970s: Discrimination against women in the workplace was common. In certain categories of work, women could legally be denied

employment if they were pregnant and unmarried; they were discriminated against when they wanted to open a credit account, or they needed their husband's or father's permission. Ivy League schools and social clubs could legally deny women access because of their biological sex.
2. The Glass Ceiling Period of the 1970s to 2000s: Significant social changes were undertaken as part of the Civil Rights Movement; the feminist era provided a sense of what was possible in terms of careers; women streamed into higher education, and this led to the phenomenon of US women today earning more undergraduate degrees than their male counterparts. The areas where women lag men in terms of numbers of students completing degrees are engineering and the sciences. But even here progress is rapidly being made.
3. The Labyrinth Period of the 2000s to today: Today we know that some women *have* made it through. There are still many, many barriers to break down. But, there are good examples and role models that we can look up to and aspire to emulate, beginning with Sallie Krawcheck, CEO of Ellevest.

Current research still reports managers and leaders being thought of as "male" rather than "female" (Cook & Glass, 2013; Swartz, 2017). Furthermore, women receive lower recognition and economic rewards for their work than men, as well as lower prestige, less knowledge, and less expertise. Accepted stereotypes depict men, not women, as having the necessary skills for leadership positions. These stereotypes continue to persist despite the fact that gender differences are not found in leadership ability (Bongiorno, Bain, & David, 2013; Hoyt, 2010; Petersen, 2016; Swartz, 2017).

In addition, research still suggests that individuals devalue women's leadership style when compared to the identical performance of men. This finding has held true since the 1960s. Deaux and Emswiller (1974) observed that equivalent performances by women and men are not explained by the same attributions. Performance by a man is attributed to skill; the identical performance by a woman is attributed to luck. When women's performance is judged by a noted authority to be superior, their performance is seen as valued. Therefore, women need to have authorities, especially men, to increase the value of her work and, by extension, of themselves (Hoyt, 2010; Swartz, 2017).

Eagly and Karau (2002) also noted that there is an incongruity between agentic leadership and femininity. Women are perceived as ineffective as leaders no matter what leadership style they use (Bongiorno et al., 2013). When women engage in behaviors stereotypically linked to men (e.g., leadership), they are not perceived similarly to men and are often evaluated more negatively than when conforming to stereotypes of women (Doyle & Paludi, 1998): According to Heilman, Wallen, Fuchs, and Tamkins (2004):

> The mere recognition that a woman has achieved success on a traditionally male task produces inferences that she has engaged in counternormative behavior and therefore causes similarly negative consequences." (p. 3)

Women will thus be perceived negatively since they are engaging in "unfeminine" behavior, referred to as the "double bind" (Denmark et al., 2008), identical to Justice Brennan's comment relating to a Catch-22 for women leaders.

According to Catalyst (2016), in the United States, 51.5% of women held management and leadership positions and 5.8% of CEO positions. In addition, women comprised 20.2% of board seats of the Fortune 500 in 2016. African-American women made up 7.9% of the board seats on the Fortune 500 that same year.

With respect to women leaders in politics, currently 21% of US Senators are women and 19.3% of US House of Representatives are women (Center for American Women and Politics, 2017). During the 2016 political campaign for President, Twitter received several comments about candidate Hillary Clinton:

> Madeline Albright: Hillary Clinton is smart, caring and determined. She is going to be an outstanding president!
>
> Ken Rayner: Assumably (sic) Bill would take on the role of "first gentleman" then. Wonder how he'll dress.
>
> Alan R. Dobson: Monica Lewinsky's ex-boyfriend's wife announces she's running for president in 2016.
>
> Jeb Bush: We must do better than Hillary. If you're committed to stopping her, add your name now.
>
> Thomas Woodrow Wilson: She's got the trustworthiness of Nixon and the warmth of an Easy Bake Oven.

As Paludi (2016) noted: when Hillary Clinton ran for President the first time in 2007, comments about a "woman President" also received media attention. Examples from a CNN.com poll (July 24, 2007) and You Tube (January 21, 2007; March 5, 2007) reported the following:

> "Hillary Clinton needs to wear a dress or skirt now and then.
>
> Her always making public appearances in pants gives a sense she is trying to "fit in" with the boys, which is never going to be the case."
>
> "Hillary is cute. Those are her qualifications for prez."
>
> "It'll be nice to have a woman president but you know white america won't let her."
>
> "Women, above all, should reject hillary. Missus clinton is the biggest misogynist of all."
>
> "...hillary clinton running must be a joke! a woman for president! HA! now thats a joke.

Pew Research Center (2015) noted that their survey on women and leadership indicated that the majority of individuals in the United States believe women are "indistinguishable" from men on leadership traits, e.g., intelligence and capacity for Innovation, and stronger than men on compassion and organization. Pew noted that four in ten survey respondents identified a double standard for women seeking leadership positions, "where they have to do more than their male counterparts to prove themselves" (p. 1). In addition, these same respondents reported doubt about whether a woman with leadership aspirations is better off having children early in her career or waiting until she is established as a leader. Twenty-two percent of respondents indicated the best option would be for women leaders not have children.

Furthermore, the White House Project (reported in Wisconsin Women's Council, 2007) noted that women seeking office do not receive "the benefit of the doubt" from voters to the same degree as men candidates. Women's use of personal biographies in their campaigns are scrutinized by voters, especially by men. Voters recommend that women political candidates avoid appearing too glamorous or too casual in their campaign material and personal appearances since both are perceived to undermine women candidates' credibility. Paludi (2016) noted that voters are also more likely to vote for women candidates when their platform involves taxes, the economy and crime. Women candidates place higher priority on equity issues and rights for women and children. In addition, women introduce most legislation dealing with women's issues (Paludi, 2016). It is important to note that once elected, women perform as well as men (Lawless & Fox, 2005).

Findings from this research highlight the necessity that work be continued to eradicate gender disparities in political office holding. In addition, media representation of women candidates and office holders has typically not been equitable (Bligh, Schlehoffer, Casad, & Gaffney, 2011; Wisconsin Women's Council, 2007). The White House Project (quoted in Wisconsin Women's Council, 2007) found in their research on six 1998 executive campaigns for positions of governor and attorney general:

1. Journalists were more likely to discuss personal characteristics of women candidates than of men (similar to the portrayal of Ms. Hopkins).
2. Unlike men, women candidates' age, marital status, family and children were covered by journalists.
3. Men received more coverage on their campaign platforms than did women.
4. Women incumbents received similar sexist coverage as women who were seeking office for the first time.

Bligh et al. (2011) reported that media has an influence on individuals' judgments of women politicians' likability, what is referred to as the "competent but cold" effect. Despite enormous progress in alerting women and men to these stereotypical portrayals, there is little debate that gender inequities continue to plague US political elections as they do in selecting women leaders in business and in the academy. Thomsen (2015) noted that the percentage of Democratic women in Congress has increased since the 1980s. However, the percentage of Republican women has stayed relatively the same. Thomsen (2015) has interpreted these statistics as indicating that Republican women have typically been to the left of their male counterparts in their political ideology and therefore not in conformity with Republican ideology.

Social stigma can explain these inequities. Social stigma is a devalued social identity that is socially discrediting; it prevents individuals from being fully accepted (Goffman, 1963). Social stigma brands individuals with an unwanted label or set of traits that remains with the individuals (Paludi, 2016). These labels or traits are typically negative and can lead to forms of social rejection, harassment, bullying and discrimination (Crocker, Major, & Steele, 1998). Eagly and Carli (2003), Paludi (2016), and Swartz (2017) reported that it is common for women to encounter discriminatory behaviors when in situations that are male-dominated (like politics and business) and when there are male-evaluators (like male voters and male senior partners). While the research suggests no modifications to this gender gap until cultural change is achieved, there are several immediate responses (Anderson et al., 2015; Lawless & Fox, 2005; Wisconsin Women's Council, 2007) including raising awareness about gender gaps through effective training programs. This volume aims to do just that.

Studies suggest women leaders embrace the following values in their work: inclusion, honesty, nurturance, participation, collaboration, communication and gender and race equity. For example, research conducted by two consulting firms, *Caliper* and *Aurora* (2005), reported that women leaders:

Are more persuasive than their male counterparts.
Learn from adversity and carry on with an "I'll show you" attitude.
Demonstrate an inclusive, team-building leadership style of problem solving and decision making.
Are likely to ignore rules and take risks.
Rodgers-Healey (2003) surveyed 193 women leaders and asked the following questions:
Do you believe that a woman can be as good a leader as a man?
Do you feel that women in a work and personal setting help each other become leaders?
What is your vision as a leader?
What forms of support do you need to make this possible?

Paludi (2016) noted that the majority of women in this research defined leadership in terms of listening, empowering others, being collaborative, facilitating change, mentoring others and being effective communicators. In addition, most of the women indicated that encouragement, equality and the presence of role models are necessary in order to achieve their visions of being good leaders.

Eagly, Johannesen-Schmidt, and van Engen (2003) further noted that for women, an effective leadership style is *transformational*, a style that incorporates empowerment, ethics, inclusiveness, nurturance, encouraging innovation and social justice. Thus, transformational leadership describes leaders who "motivate subordinates to transcend their own self-interests for the good of the group or organization" (Powell, Butterfield, & Bartol, 2008, p. 159). Burns (1978) described transformational leadership as occurring "…when one or more persons engage with others in such a way that leaders and followers raise one another to higher levels of motivation and morality…transforming leadership ultimately becomes moral in that it raises the level of human conduct and ethical aspirations of both the leader and led, and thus, has a transforming effect on both."

In contrast, *transactional* leaders form exchange relationships through using rewards and punishment as incentives for employee performance. Transactional leadership is associated with aggression (Powell et al., 2008). According to Duff-McCall and Schweinle (2008), a transactional leadership "…suits the masculine social interaction and leadership style, because men internalize the male gender role, which supports an agentic desire for competition, aggression, and assertion" (p. 90). Thus, transactional leadership rewards competition, aggression and an authoritarian managerial style (Eagly & Johannesen-Schmidt, 2001). Eagly et al. (2003) found women score higher than men on only one aspect of transactional leadership that is related to positive outcomes: rewarding their employees for good performance. Thus, women who are transformational leaders exhibit their caring and nurturing toward employees through praise and other forms of rewards.

The research on transformational leadership styles would predict that women, who are more likely to use this style should not face any barriers to becoming leaders. However, women experience significant barriers, including dealing with gatekeepers, pay inequity, lack of work/life integration and harassment/discrimination, which keep them from reaching their full potential as leaders. Eagly and Karau (2002) and Swartz (2017) noted that there is an incongruity between agentic leadership and femininity.

Jandeska and Kraimer (2005) found that most organizations are structured by traditional and stereotypical masculine culture which values and rewards men who exhibit these stereotypical traits more so than women. Women struggle to find their place within these organizations. According to Jandeska and Kraimer (2005):

> This "code of conduct" in masculine cultures, while recognizable to males, can be completely alien to females and thus would be considered less hospitable towards women's careers. For example, an "old-boy network" excludes women from centers of influence and valuable sources of information, often trivializing or ignoring their contributions. (p. 465)

Jandeska and Kraimer (2005) further found that collective organizational cultures exist that reward more stereotypic feminine behaviors. These collectivistic cultures focus on cooperation and empowerment. They are conducive to women being more satisfied with their careers and more engaged to the organization's success. As Jandeska and Kraimer (2005) noted:

> Even women in senior roles in large corporations find themselves "on the outside looking in" when it comes to information sharing and access to the inner circle, where decisions are made.... Women characterize such a culture as exclusionary and claim that upper management often lacks awareness of the barriers it creates to women's assimilation and advancement. (p. 465)

Yoder (2001) also noted that a transformational leadership style would be perceived as effective in "a congenial setting," one in which empowering and nurturing subordinates is valued. Denmark et al. (2008) further suggested that organizations must be supportive of transformational leadership "...by legitimizing and encouraging women leaders and by ensuring that the male/female ratio of employees is not skewed in favor of male employees" (p. 38).

Margaret Chesney (2007) once quipped with regard to women and leadership: "The ceiling is breaking—but watch out for falling glass." Nevertheless, the breaking up of the glass ceiling, is still slow, and this has led Eagly and Carli (2007) to create a more updated metaphor—the *labyrinth*. This metaphor captures the multiple complex challenges, false starts, and barriers that women encounter as they navigate the lanes to leadership victories in the twenty-first century. It is our hope that this book serves as a (wo)mentor for women aspiring to become leaders. We echo the sentiment of Denmark et al. (2008) who recommend the following to empower women to become leaders:

> ...women should band together and actively participate in groups that unite women. Whether this be a union or a group of women within a department, it has been through this

action of uniting and supporting that women have made progress in the past and which provides a key to progress in the future' (p. 54).

This book on women and leadership features scholarly research about work environments that welcome women leaders and those that served as gatekeepers, preventing them from being leaders. Contributors discuss women leaders' continued struggle to break the glass ceiling, social stigma attached to women leaders, implicit bias, sexism and racism in hiring and evaluating leaders in organizations. We take a multicultural approach to women and leadership. We also offer readers resources on women's leadership institutes, organizations concerned with women and leadership and global feminist leadership programs.

In addition, we feature personal accounts from women in organizations about their experiences as leaders and with women leaders. This idiographic approach (Paludi & Fankell-Hauser, 1986) to understanding women's leadership styles and experiences illustrates how women differ in the strength of their striving for achieving leadership and in the roles that elicit this striving. These personal accounts also highlight organizational factors and personal factors that facilitated or hindered women leaders' career development. These personal accounts stimulate additional research agendas on women and leadership that make women leaders central, not marginal and visible, not invisible.

Albany, NY, USA Michele A. Paludi
New York, NY, USA Florence L. Denmark

References

Anderson, A., Ahmad, A., King, E., Lindsey, A., Feyre, R., Ragone, S., & Kim, S. (2015). The effectiveness of three strategies to reduce the influence of bias in evaluations of female leaders. *Journal of Applied Social Psychology, 45*, 522–539.

Bligh, M., Schlehoffer, M, Casad, B., & Gaffney, A. (2011). Competent enough, but would you vote for her? Gender stereotypes and media influences on perceptions of women politicians. *Journal of Applied Social Psychology, 42*, 560–597.

Bongiorno, R., Bain, P., & David, B. (2013). If you're going to be a leader, at least act like it! Prejudice towards women who are tentative in leader roles. *British Journal of Social Psychology, 53*, 217–234.

Caliper. (2005). *Women leaders study: The qualities that distinguish women leaders*. Retrieved May 13, 2010, from http://www.caliperonline.com/brochures/WomenLeaderWhitePaper.pdf.

Catalyst. (2016). *Women in leadership*. Retrieved August 14, 2017, from http://www.catalyst.org/knowledge/topics/women-leadership.

Center for American Women and Politics (2017). *Facts: Current numbers and historical data on women in politics*. Retrieved on April 8, 2018 from http://www.cawp.rutgers.edu/facts.

Chesney, M. (2007, September). *Women in leadership-the ceiling is breaking...but watch out for falling glass*. Paper presented at the meeting of the Committee on Women in Psychology Leadership Institute for Women in Psychology: Qualitative evaluation of training needs. Washington, DC.

Cook, A., & Glass, C. (2013). Women and top leadership positions: Towards an institutional analysis. *Gender, Work, and Organization, 21*, 91–103.

Crocker, J., Major, B., & Steele, C. (1998). Social stigma. In D. T. Gilbert & S. T. Fiske (Eds.), *Handbook of social psychology* (4th ed., pp. 504–553). New York, NY: McGraw-Hill.
Denmark, F., Baron, E., Klara, M., SIgal, J., Gibbs, M., & Wnuk, D. (2008). Women as leaders: From the lab to the real world. In M. Paludi (Ed.), *The psychology of women at work: Challenges and solutions for our female workforce* (pp. 35–56). Westport, CT: Praeger.
Deaux, K., & Emswiller, T. (1974). Explanations of successful performance in sex-linked tasks: What is skill for the male is luck for the female. *Journal of Personality and Social Psychology, 29*, 80–85.
Doyle, J., & Paludi, M. (1998). *Sex and gender.* New York, NY: McGraw-Hill.
Duff-McCall, K., & Schweinle, W. (2008). Leadership and women. In M. Paludi (Ed.), *The psychology of women at work: Challenges and solutions for our female workforce* (pp. 87–99). Westport, CT: Praeger.
Eagly, A., & Carli, L. (2007) *Through the labyrinth: The truth about how women become leaders.* Boston, MA: Harvard Business School Press.
Eagly, A., & Johannesen-Schmidt, M. (2001). The leadership styles of women and men. *Journal of Social Issues, 57,* 781–797.
Eagly, A., Johannesen-Schmidt, M., & vanENgen, M. (2003). Transformation, transactional and laissez-faire leadership styles: A meta-analysis comparing women and men. *Psychological Bulletin, 108*, 233–256.
Eagly, A., & Karau, S. (2002). Role congruity theory of prejudice toward female leaders. *Psychological Review, 109,* 573–598.
Goffman, E. (1963). *Stigma: Notes on the management of spoiled identity.* New York, NY: Simon & Schuster.
Heilman, M., Wallen, A., Fuchs, D., & Tamkins, M. (2004). Penalties for success: Reactions to women who succeed at male gender-typed tasks. *Journal of Applied Psychology, 74,* 935–942.
Hoyt, C. (2010). Women, men, and leadership: Exploring the gender gap at the top. *Social and Personality Psychology Compass, 4*, 484–498.
Jandeska, K., & Kraimer, M. (2005). Women's perceptions of organizational culture, work attitudes, and role-modeling behaviors. *Journal of Managerial Issues, 18*, 461–478.
Lawless, J., & Fox, R. (2005). *Men rule: The continued under-representation of women in U.S. politics.* Washington, DC: Women and Politics Institute.
Levit, N. (1998). *The gender line: Men, women, and the law.* New York, NY: New York University Press.
Paludi, M. (Ed.). (2016). *Why Congress needs women.* Santa Barbara, CA: Praeger.
Paludi, M., & Fankell-Hauser, J. (1986). An idiographic approach to the study of women's achievement strivings. *Psychology of Women Quarterly, 10,* 89–100.
Pew Research Center. (2015). *Women and leadership.* Retrieved August 14, 2017, from http://www.pewsocialtrends.org/2015/01/14/women-and-leadership/.
Powell, G., Butterfield, D., & Bartol, K. (2008). Leader evaluations: A new female advantage? *Gender in Management: An International Journal, 23,* 156–174.
Price Waterhouse v. Hopkins, 490 U.S. 228, at 234.
Rodgers-Healey, D. (2003). *12 insights into leadership for women.* Retrieved May 13, 2010, from www.leadershipforwomen.com.au.
Swartz, E. (2017, May). *Making it through the labyrinth: Gender bias in management.* Paper presented at Excelsior College, Albany, New York.
Thomsen, D. (2015). Why so few (Republican) women? Explaining the partisan imbalance of women in the U.S. Congress. *Legislative Studies Quarterly, 40*, 295–323.
Wachs Book, W. (2001). *Why the best man for the job is a woman: The unique female qualities of leadership.* New York, NY: Harper Collins.
Wisconsin Women's Council. (2007). *Who me? What we know about why women don't run for political office.*
Yoder, J. (2001). Strategies for change: Making leadership work more effectively for women. *Journal of Social Issues, 57,* 815–828.

Acknowledgments

Florence extends her thanks to all the past and future women leaders in psychology.

Michele thanks her sisters, Rosalie and Lucille, for their support.

Michele is appreciative of colleagues in the Lean-In Circle she has co-moderated with Noelle Kendrick at Excelsior College: Noelle Kendrick, Lisa LaVigna, Dale Emeagwali, Amber O'Neil, Mark Howe, Cathy Kushner, Leigh Tedesco, Areatha Fryer. She also expresses her thanks to Katie Hammer for providing quotations about women leaders. Michele also thanks students in her human resources course at Clarkson University, Capital Region Campus: Morgan Seber, Reese Bernal, Derrick Tusang, Tyler Dehmer, Casey MacClaren, and Benjamin Bucinell. Michele expresses her thanks to Erin Vitali and Hem Borromeo, her mentees for the Excelsior College Leadership Academy.

Contents

Editors Biographies

Florence L. Denmark Florence L. Denmark is an internationally recognized scholar and policy maker. She received her PhD in Social Psychology from the University of Pennsylvania and has six honorary degrees and numerous awards, including one for Outstanding Lifetime Contributions to Psychology. Denmark is a Distinguished Research Professor of Psychology at Pace University. A past president of the American Psychological Association (APA), Eastern Psychological Association (EPA), Psi Chi, and International Council of Psychologists (ICP), Denmark holds fellowship status in the APA, EPA, Association for Psychological Science (APS), International Association for Applied Psy chol ogy (IAAP), and Society for Experimental Social Psychology (SESP). Denmark is currently the main NGO representative to the United Nations (UN) for the ICP as well as a UN representative for the IAAP. She is co-chair of the UN CoNGO Family Committee and as well as a past chair of the UN CoNGO Executive Committee of Ageing. Denmark's most significant research and extensive publications have emphasized women's leadership and leadership styles, the interaction of status and gender, ageing women in cross-cultural perspective, and the history of women in psychology.

Michele A. Paludi Michele A. Paludi, PhD, is series editor for Praeger's series in Women's Psychology, the author/editor of 56 college textbooks and more than 250 scholarly articles and conference presentations on human resource management, leadership, workplace discrimination, diversity and inclusivity, sexual harassment, campus/workplace violence, and the psychology of women. Paludi serves as an expert witness for court proceedings and administrative hearings. She has had extensive experience in conducting training programs and investigations of Equal Employment Opportunity (EEO) issues for businesses and educational institutions. She is the Senior Faculty Program Director in the School of Business and Technology and the Faculty Program Director for Human Resources and Leadership at Excelsior College.

Contributors Biographies

Joseph Angiello Joseph Angiello has served as the chair for the Master of Arts in Business and Policy Studies program as well as chair for the Master of Arts in Social Policy program at the State University of New York at Empire State College. Currently, he serves as the coordinator of the new Master of Arts in Community and Economic Development program and as coordinator for the Advanced Graduate Certificate programs in Nonprofit Management and Social Entrepreneurship. He is an associate professor with a dual appointment in Empire State College's MBA program and Policy Studies program. Prior to Empire State College, Dr. Angiello served in a variety of faculty and administrative positions in other colleges. Dr. Angiello has earned a Ph.D. in higher education administration from The University of Texas at Austin and a master of arts degree in economics from Fordham University's Graduate School of Arts and Sciences. He has also completed advanced management study at George Washington University.

Bryan T. Baldwin Bryan T. Baldwin has been CEO of a recording company, CEO of a publishing company, led national and global sales teams for Fortune 500 companies, and has a passion for growing sales and revenue channels. He and Frank Wilkerson have developed a proven sales process that has generated millions of dollars in revenue for Fortune ranked companies. Bryan completed his Doctorate in Business Administration. His dissertation was focused on talent management strategies and revenue generation in Fortune 500 companies. He is a founding member of Leaders Excellence Harvard Square and has been inducted into the prestigious Delta Mu Delta Honor Society for Business Administration. Bryan was proclaimed Outstanding Georgia Citizen by Secretary of State Brian Kemp for his business and civic contributions to the state of Georgia.

Maryann Bastnagel Maryann Bastnagel has a diverse professional background that includes a unique blend of experiences, serving as an executive in traditional, Fortune 100 companies and as an entrepreneur, and starting a number of businesses from scratch. She served as a Chief Information Officer (CIO) and Chief Technology Officer (CTO) for several world-class companies, including Marriott International,

Time Warner/AOL, Fannie Mae and the Airline Tariff Publishing Corporation (ATPCO). She has been a founder and operational executive in several successful start-ups and entrepreneurial ventures including Travel Services International, where she served as the CIO and President of the e-Travel division. Earning a B.A. in Communications and a B.S. in Engineering/Information Technology Management from the University of Maryland, Maryann is also a graduate of the Marriott Executive Leadership program via the Robert H. Smith Business School at the University of Maryland. She holds three patents in the subject of "Big Data": two for data mining of customer information to determine purchase preferences and one for the management of financial loan data. Maryann is a graduate of the Coaching Certification program at The Hudson Institute of Coaching, the industry leader in executive coaching and is certified by the International Coach Federation at the Professional Certified Coach (PCC) level. She coaches individuals who wish to enhance their impact and excel in expanded or different roles, as well as those who are in periods of career transition. Maryann also serves as the Chairman of the Board for the Economic Development Corporation for Hilton Head Island, South Carolina. She also serves on the Board of the Community Services Association (CSA) for the Sea Pines community in Hilton Head Island, South Carolina.

Alan Belasen Alan Belasen holds a Ph.D. from Rockefeller College, SUNY. For over 25 years, Dr. Belasen has been involved in executive education and development programs in the U.S. and abroad in startups, business enterprises, multinational companies, nonprofits, government agencies, academic institutions, and healthcare organizations. Dr. Belasen chaired the MBA Program at SUNY, Empire State College from 2004 to 2015 where he designed and supervised the implementation of the MBA in Management; MBA in Global Leadership, MBA in Healthcare Leadership, and MBA Pathway for Veterans. Currently he is leading the development of the Doctorate in Business Administration. Dr. Belasen has written over 120 journal articles, book chapters and conference papers on topics such as executive education, self-managed work teams; HR competencies; work motivation; women's leadership; communication innovation, corruption in business, trusted leadership, healthcare curriculum, healthcare management, and leadership development. His articles appear in *The Journal of Health Administration Education, Leadership & Organization Development Journal*; *Journal of Human Resource Management*; *International Journal of Human Resources Development and Management*; *The Atlantic Journal of Communication; The International Journal of Leadership Studies, Journal of Economic Modeling; Journal of Management Development;* and the *Proceedings of the Academy of Management*. Alan Belasen's books include*: Leading the Learning Organization: Communication and Competencies for Managing Change* (SUNY Press, 2000); *The Theory and Practice of Corporate Communication: A Competing Values Perspective* (Sage, 2008); *Developing Women Leaders in Corporate America: Balancing Competing Demands, Transcending Traditional Boundaries* (Praeger, 2012*); Mastering Leadership: A Vital Resource for Healthcare Managers* (Jones & Bartlett Learning, 2015); *Confronting Corruption in Business: Trusted Leadership, Civic*

Engagement (Routledge (2016); and, *Women in Management: A Framework for Sustainable Work-life Integration* (Routledge, 2017).

Chloe E. Bortmas Chloe E. Bortmas, was a student and research assistant of French and education at the University of Mount Union. As a research assistant, she worked on several projects based on feminism, gender, and race. One of her works includes the curriculum for Kappa Delta Pi, *Culturally Responsive Teaching and Leading Conference* (2016) which examines culturally responsive pedagogy for teachers in the classroom. Her current chapter, "Focus Group becomes Support Group: Women in Educational Leadership" (appearing in this volume), stems from her research with Jennifer L. Martin and Martina Sharp Grier based on the challenges that women face in leadership positions.

Andrea Diese Andrea Diese is the Chief Operating Officer for Sterling Marketing, Management and Consulting where she excels at strategic planning and implementation and is able to incorporate her passion and 20 years of knowledge in training and development. Previously, Dr. Diese worked in administration at the University level for several years as a College Chair for the School of Business. Some of her responsibilities included leading the selection, assessment, certification, mentoring, evaluation and training of campus faculty. In addition, she developed and maintained the quality and integrity of the College's Programs. Prior to transiting to higher education, Dr. Diese worked as the Training and Development Manager for US Army in the Project Management Defense Communication and Army Switched Systems division. She supported the warfighter by providing technical support to the Product Manager, Defense Communications Systems Continental United States (PM-DCS CONUS—Continental United States and SWA—Southwest Asia) office by analyzing and defining Directorate of Information Management (DOIM) training requirements, developing training strategies, identifying training sources, and coordinating training. Some of her responsibilities included organizational assessments that entailed succession planning, knowledge transference, reengineering and change initiatives, utilizing continuous improvement and document training procedures to maintain effectiveness and efficiencies within the agency, and perform metric evaluations to ensure the to alignment of tasks to the vision, mission, strategic goals and objectives of the organization. Dr. Diese holds a Doctorate of Management in Organizational Leadership and a Master of Arts in Organizational Management from the University of Phoenix and a Bachelor of Arts in Business Management and Spanish from Moravian College in Bethlehem, Pennsylvania.

John A. Gallien John A. Gallien is a graduate student at the University of Texas at Tyler. He received his B.A. in Psychology from San Diego State University and is currently receiving his M.S. in Clinical Psychology with a focus on Neuropsychology. Additionally, he has worked as a counselor in a variety of mental health settings and continues to expand the breadth of his mental health expertise.

Joyce Henderson Joyce Henderson teaches and consults in the areas of human resources, strategic planning, leadership, transformational learning, design and facilitation of learning in the virtual classroom. Dr. Henderson is a former Human Resources executive for Marriott International, the national vice president of human resources for Volunteers of America, Inc. and has taught for over 15 years. In addition, she has served on numerous boards of directors, councils and advisory boards for a variety of for profit and nonprofit organizations. Serving as an adjunct professor in the graduate schools at The Catholic University of America and Excelsior College, she teaches in the face to face, hybrid and on line format. The topic areas of crisis communications, strategic planning of human resources, conflict resolution and leadership are among her courses. In addition, she assists with instructional design and faculty development. She also continues her research and publication interests of transformational learning in the online classroom while being keenly interested in the impact of the continuous evolution of information technology on higher education, learning and communication. Holding a MBA from the University of North Texas in Denton, Texas and a doctorate from The George Washington University in Washington, DC, Joyce resides in Silver Spring, Maryland. Enjoying the DC area, she also includes frequent visits to her home state of Texas where she has a second residence in the small East Texas town of Linden. There she is active in several revitalization efforts such as Main Street, USA and efforts to preserve the rich musical and other heritage of the town including among others, the oldest continuously operating courthouse in the state and a 1930s historic firehouse.

Jennifer Ledesma Jennifer Ledesma earned her BA in Psychology from Hunter College of the City University of New York. She has worked with low-income families at New York University's Steinhardt Center for Research on Culture, Development and Education and continues to promote early literacy and school readiness for NYC children through The Video Interaction Project's hospital based parenting intervention. Jennifer is currently a doctoral student in School and Clinical Psychology at Pace University. Her research interests include cultural differences in parenting styles and the impact on children's cognitive, social and emotional development. Her experience working with children and families has inspired further interest in women's issues of equality and leadership.

Krystal Lozada Krystal Lozada is a recent graduate from Queens College of the City University of New York and is in her last year as a Master of Arts student at Pace University in New York, studying psychology. She is a past Intern at the United Nations for the International Council of Psychologists and is currently an Associate Member of ICP for the UN team. Krystal has a special interest in research with a focus on gender studies, mental health and social behavior. She plans to pursue a PhD in Clinical Psychology.

Paula K. Lundberg-Love Paula K. Lundberg-Love is a professor of psychology at the University of Texas at Tyler (UTT) where she teaches psychopharmacology, behavioral neuroscience, physiological psychology, sexual victimization, and family violence. Dr. Lundberg-Love is also a licensed professional counselor at Tyler Counseling and Assessment Center in Tyler, where she provides therapeutic services for victims of sexual assault, child sexual abuse and domestic violence. Her research interests have focused on the treatment of women with histories of incestuous abuse. She is the author of nearly 200 publications and presentations and is co-editor of *Violence and Sexual Abuse at Home: Current Issues in Spousal Battering and Child Maltreatment*, *Intimate Violence Against Women: When Spouses, Partners, or Lovers Attack* and *Women and Mental Disorders.*

Jennifer L. Martin Jennifer L. Martin is an assistant professor of education at the University of Mount Union. Prior to working in higher education, Dr. Martin worked in public education for 17 years, 15 of those as the department chair of English at an urban alternative high school for students labeled at-risk for school failure in metropolitan Detroit. She is the editor of the two-volume series Women as Leaders in Education: Succeeding Despite Inequity, Discrimination, and Other Challenges (Praeger, 2011) which examines the intersections of class, race, gender, and sexuality for current and aspiring leaders from a variety of perspectives. Dr. Martin's current book project is Racial Battle Fatigue: Insights from the Front Lines of Social Justice Advocacy, which contains personal stories of the repercussions of doing social justice work in the field and in the university (Recipient of the 2016 AERA Division B's Outstanding Book Recognition Award). Dr. Martin has numerous publications on bullying and harassment, educational equity, and issues of social justice, including: Rowman & Littlefield entitled Teaching for educational equity: Case studies for professional development and principal preparation, volumes 1 (2016) and 2 (2017), and Feminist pedagogy, practice, and activism: Improving lives for girls and women (Routledge, 2017). She is currently studying the development of culturally responsive leadership practices.

Sharlyn Moore Sharlyn Moore is the President and CEO for Sterling Marketing, Management and Consulting. Previous to launching her own business, Dr. Moore directed the marketing initiatives and membership growth for the National Club Association (NCA), a non-profit lobby group established to protect the best interest of the Private Club Industry. Before NCA, she managed the global customer advocacy programs for Verizon Business Information Security Solutions. During her tenure with Verizon Business, she was responsible for leading and developing global strategic customer programs across a variety of marketing initiatives, which included the development and execution of Customer Advisory Boards, as well as leveraging customer content across a variety of channels. Prior to Verizon Business, Dr. Moore held a variety of roles within the hospitality industry to include vice president of operations, regional director of sales and marketing, and director of operations. In addition to a specialization in all aspects of operations, sales, and marketing, she assumed the fiscal responsibilities of overseeing multi-million dollar budgets, property renovations, large project management assignments, strategic marketing plan development, and the execution through various integrated marketing and public relations initiatives. Dr. Moore obtained her Doctorate in Management &

Organizational Leadership from the University of Phoenix and M.S. degree in Clinical and Counseling Psychology; B.S. degree in Psychology; and B.A. degree in Biology (Pre-med) from Abilene Christian University in Abilene, Texas.

Wendy Murphy Wendy Murphy has served as adjunct professor of sexual violence law at New England Law|Boston, where she also codirects the Women's and Children's Advocacy Project under the Center for Law and Social Responsibility. A former Visiting Scholar at Harvard Law School, Wendy prosecuted child abuse and sex crimes cases for many years. In 1992 she founded the first organization in the nation to provide pro bono legal services to crime victims. Wendy writes and lectures widely on the constitutional and civil rights of women and children, and criminal justice policy. She is a contributing editor for The Sexual Assault Report, and writes a regular column for The Patriot Ledger. Wendy has published numerous scholarly articles including a landmark law review article explaining the legal relationship between sexual assault on campus and Title IX.She regularly provides legal analysis for network and cable news programs. Her first book, "And Justice For Some," was published by Penguin/S.

Divya A. Patel Divya A. Patel is a Clinical Neuropsychology graduate student at the University of Texas at Tyler where she is a research assistant in the Memory Assessment and Research Center and the Social Emotions and Motivation Laboratory. Divya plans to pursue a doctoral degree Clinical Neuropsychology.

Diane L. Rothberg Diane L. Rothberg has worked as both a Journalist and a Professional Pilot. She earned her Bachelor of Journalism from Carleton University, Ottawa, Canada in 1974. When she joined the University Sport Parachuting club, she became fascinated with airplanes, and had over 200 takeoffs in an airplane before she ever landed in one. When her father forbade her to fly take up flying, she immediately enrolled in flight school. What started as an act of rebellion quickly became a passion, and eventually evolved into a profession. She has been a Flight instructor, Corporate Pilot, Bush Pilot and an Aviation Safety Officer for Transport Canada, where she was Editor of an aviation safety publication which was distributed to all licensed pilots in the country. In 1985 she realized her dream of flying for Air Canada, the nation's flag carrier, where she enjoyed an exciting and fulfilling career as an airline pilot on the B-727, L1011, DC-9, B-767 and Airbus A320 aircraft. She is now retired, and living in Gainesville, Georgia.

Gavin D. Sanders Gavin D. Sanders is currently in the final year of his master's program in clinical psychology with a specialization in neuropsychology. His primary research interests involve neurodegenerative diseases, specifically traumatic brain injury and dementia, as well as the neuropsychological assessment of those populations. He has been involved in various research projects during both his undergraduate and graduate programs. Gavin plans to pursue his doctorate in Clinical Neuropsychology.

Martina L. Sharp-Grier Martina L. Sharp-Grier is an Assistant Professor and Department Coordinator of Sociology and Gerontology at Stark State College, in North Canton, OH and a Certified Equity Consultant for The National Alliance for Partnerships in Equity (NAPE). She has a long history of public service, having been employed as a probation officer for the Montgomery County Ohio Adult Probation Department, and as a parole officer for the State of Ohio Adult Parole Authority. She has also maintained professional positions in victim advocacy and forensic social work. As an educator, Sharp-Grier has designed and taught courses in sociology, social problems, sex and gender, and racial and ethnic relations. While she previously held a Lecturer of Women's Studies assignment at a 4-year research university, her current position at a 2-year college allows her to work passionately with nontraditional students—first time/full-time scholars and students representing underserved populations. Her passion for these communities is special, as this student population is illustrative of her personal narrative. She feels passionately that providing a venue where students can critically analyze and study their milieu is key in preparing them for productive citizenship. Sharp-Grier's research is interdisciplinary and utilizes qualitative inquiry through Autoethnography, Indigenous Cultural Research methods, and Critical Performance Pedagogy. Her areas of inquiry include racial and gendered identity formation and maintenance, inequalities within the social structure related to race, sex, and sexuality, microaggressions in higher education, domestic violence/intimate partner violence, sexual harassment—both virtual and direct, and bullying in the workplace as correlated with minority status. In addition to multiple single and co-authored publications and projects, she is co-editor of the anthology, *Feminist Pedagogy, Practice, and Activism: Improving the Lives of Girls and Women*, which was released by Routledge Press in 2017.

Cortni D. Smith Cortni D. Smith is a graduate student in the Clinical Neuropsychology program at the University of Texas at Tyler where she is studying Neuropsychological Assessment and is interested in working with patients with traumatic brain injury. Subsequent to completion of her Master of Science degree, Cortni plans to pursue her Ph.D. in Clinical Neuropsychology.

Savannah White Savannah White is an Academic Advisor at Excelsior College specializing in the nursing and health sciences degree programs. Previously, Savannah worked as a Student Success Coach using coaching methodologies and relational skills that empowered students to achieve their goals and become the best versions of themselves. She has 10 years of higher education administration experience and graduated from the State University of New York at New Paltz with a bachelors in Management. In 2017, Savannah graduated from Excelsior College with a masters of science in Management with a concentration in organizational leadership.

Frank Wilkerson Frank Wilkerson has been a CEO, Executive Director, and President of various companies for over 20 years. His various roles have demanded expertise in both regional, national and international business. For almost a decade, he has been responsible for leading and developing a regional, national and international sales team and strategy catering to F500 companies. As a Vice President and a member of a Senior Leadership team he has collaborated with Bryan Baldwin, to develop not only a top notch sales team but a strategy that has proven successful in producing millions in revenue year over year within the F500 community. Frank has earned a Doctorate with an emphasis in Education/Administration, a Masters in Counseling/Administration and a Bachelors in Psychology/Sociology. He is also a graduate of the Naval Post Graduate School (Foreign Language Institute) with an emphasis on Foreign Languages.

Contributors

Joseph Angiello MBA Program, SUNY Empire State College, Saratoga Springs, NY, USA

Bryan T. Baldwin Cumming, GA, USA

Maryann Bastnagel Bethesda, MA, USA

Alan Belasen MBA Program, SUNY Empire State College, Saratoga Springs, NY, USA

Chloe E. Bortmas Alliance, OH, USA

Florence L. Denmark Department of Psychology, Pace University, New York, NY, USA

Andrea Diese American College of Commerce and Technology, Falls Church, VA, USA

John A. Gallien University of Texas at Tyler, Tyler, TX, USA

Joyce Henderson University of Maryland, Silver Spring, MD, USA

Jennifer Ledesma Pace University, New York, NY, USA

Krystal Lozada Pace University, New York, NY, USA

Paula K. Lundberg-Love University of Texas at Tyler, Tyler, TX, USA

Jennifer L. Martin Alliance, OH, USA

Sharlyn Moore Sterling Marketing Management & Consulting, Stephens City, VA, USA

Wendy Murphy New England Law Boston, Boston, MA, USA

Divya A. Patel University of Texas at Tyler, Tyler, TX, USA

Diane L. Rothberg Gainesville, GA, USA

Michele A. Paludi Excelsior College, Albany, GA, USA

Gavin D. Sanders University of Texas at Tyler, Tyler, TX, USA

Martina L. Sharp-Grier North Canton, OH, USA

Cortni D. Smith University of Texas at Tyler, Tyler, TX, USA

Frank Wilkerson Cumming, GA, USA

Turn Ah-Ha Moments into Pivotal Learning

Joyce Henderson and Maryann Bastnagel

Some leaders are born women.

Geraldine Ferraro

Introduction

Many theories exist about women in leadership roles (as evidenced in the chapters that are included in this book). From our own professional experiences, we believe that continuous learning is essential as leaders in that, as Newport (2016) points out, if you can't learn, you can't thrive. We believe this to be true not only in our own lives but also in those of the women leaders we know, observed, and interviewed. Further, we have come to realize that learning resulting in pivotal changes most often begin with an ah-ha moment which serves as the catalyst or trigger. We have noted, however, that many find evidence of the ah-ha moment being formed over time and not fully recognized until the one moment when the realization is asserted.

We have observed that in order for the ah-ha moment to lead to a pivotal change in our thinking, we need to embrace it, take time to critically reflect on it, and dialogue with another about it before it can be reflected as a change in our thinking and/or behavior. Unfortunately, as the distractions in our abundantly connected and plugged in world increase, we do not always take the time to face what the ah-ha moment is telling us. When we do critically reflect and consider accepting the changes, we are learning, thriving, and being at our best as leaders. Sometimes the learning results in small changes but at times it is so significant that it can result in transformational learning (Mezirow, 1991). We saw evidence of transformational

J. Henderson (✉)
University of Maryland, Silver Spring, MD, USA

M. Bastnagel
Bethesda, MA, USA

F. L. Denmark, M. A. Paludi (eds.), *Women and Leadership*,
https://doi.org/10.1007/978-3-319-72182-8_1

learning in the examples of the women who participated in our interviews for this chapter in the book which brings us to the major premises that we put forward in this chapter which are threefold and include the following:

1. Pivotal learning begins with a realization that our thinking needs assessing which can enhance our ability to thrive and lead in an even more effective manner.
2. We can foster an opportunity for pivotal learning for others. As one person in our research stated, "if you want to change a person's thinking on something, you need to provide them with a new way of thinking."
3. We must make the space for mindful critical thinking in our lives. We must unplug.

Methodology of Research and Underlying Theory

Our methodology was simple. We interviewed six women ranging in age from 30 to 70 of our own acquaintance, using a semi-structured interview approach (Bernard, 1988). We did not include all the experiences that were shared because they were so plentiful. We also drew upon our own experiences as organizational leaders.

Graphic 1

The knowledge for our study is informed by the work of Mezirow (1991) who devoted his life's research to what he referred to as transformative learning. In his body of work, he found that the transformation in our ways of thinking begins with a disorienting dilemma. For the purposes of this chapter, we refer to this as the ah-ha moment which can manifest in what Mezirow (1991) named transformative learning. We refer to this as a pivotal change (or learning) in our thinking or about our behavior. Our research is also informed by Feslinger (1957) whose published theory of cognitive dissonance is useful for our look at ah-ha moments because it helps us to understand why while the changes that occur can be powerful in changing the whole order for how we think, that change can also be painful and perhaps resisted or ignored.

Mezirow (1991) explains the process (depicted in graphic 2) of how we change our thinking, beliefs, and the way we see the world (and ourselves) in it. He explains that the process typically begins with a trigger, followed by critical reflection, discourse with another (or others), and assimilating the new thinking into action. Interestingly, his research began as he noticed his wife (after returning to college after being a stay at home mom for a number of years), expressing new thoughts and ideas (differing from her previous thinking) about roles she and other women could take. This obvious change interested her husband and what followed was his life-long research about the process for transformative learning. We briefly describe the four segments of the process as follows.

Graphic 2

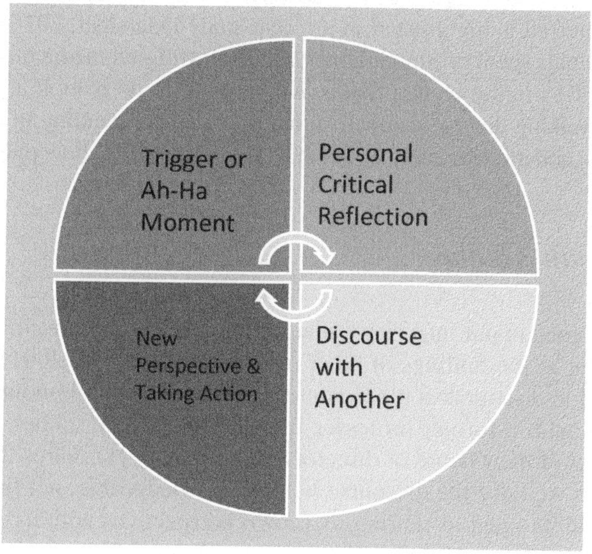

Trigger

The trigger for the ah-ha moment is at times a sudden experience but we have also observed that, upon critical reflection of our past experiences, there exists a more gradual or iterative process. In our recent interviews with women leaders we found both. We heard about triggers coming from sudden experiences such as a 360-degree feedback, attendance at professional conferences, workshops or seminars, board meetings, conversations with mentors and coaches; and we also learned that in some cases the inner voice or thoughts had been as one woman stated, remunerating, for a long while. Another discovered the gradual or iterative thinking taking place only after reading their personal blog or journal.

Critical Reflection

The importance of critical reflection is explained by Mezirow (2011) as it requires a hiatus in which to reassess one's meaning perspectives and, if necessary, to transform them. Critical reflection is not concerned with the how or the how-to of action, but with the why, the reasons for and the consequences of what we do. We offer in the last segment of this chapter some suggestions for building the time for critical reflection into our lives but we realize it is not easy given the many distractions and need to be connected. In a Ted Talks presentation, Turkler (2008) stated that being so connected all the time to our smartphones, email, and social media concerns her because she thinks we are setting ourselves up for trouble in how we relate to each other, but also trouble in how we relate to ourselves and our capacity for self-reflection. This propensity to always be connected is highlighted in a recent study (Marshall, 2015) reporting that the time individuals spent on smartphones consuming digital media increased by 90% from 2013 to 2015 in the United States. All we have to do is look around at people texting while walking down the street, sitting in meetings, standing in checkout lines, at dinner tables, and unfortunately even while driving to realize how plugged in we are.

Discourse with Another

Most of the women in our interviews shared examples of their discourse with others that was similar to the findings of other research (Henderson, 2001) revealing that CEOs engaged in discourse at the Conference Board's CEO Roundtable, with executive coaches, with a former professor from their graduate school program and a trusted member of their board of directors. Mezirow (1991) shares that the individual with whom we have the discourse will be knowledgeable, not hold power over or under us and be open to sharing their own perspectives with us. There must be candor and truth.

Action

The action, referred to in the fourth portion of the process depicted in graphic 2, is as unique as the individual. Action will typically manifest in how decisions are made, how situations are approached, the roles that are taken on, or how we view ourselves and our competencies. Others typically notice a difference in the individual's conversation, how they make decisions or respond to others. Following are examples of pivotal changes of women leaders we interviewed. We have given the women fictitious names in order to personalize them and their fantastic experiences.

The Pivotal Learning Experiences

There are various scenarios when the ah-ha moment occurs. There are also various responses to it (that is, what one does with the learning). This section shares examples of the *when* and the *what* (when it happened and what the individuals did that resulted in some transformation).

Transitioning from Engineer to Manager

A woman leader in the field of information technology, Jane shared a pivotal moment that provided the basis for a critical turning point in her career. Jane was one of a small number of female engineers working in a hard core engineering division for IBM in the 1980s. She led a team of approximately 20 systems programmers and architects, mostly men, who were responsible for the successful development and operation of hundreds of systems for IBM's customers. Jane was invited to participate in a management development seminar for IBM's high potential leaders, a program that included individuals from the engineering discipline, as well as professionals in sales, marketing, and customer account services. During the seminar, the facilitator introduced a problem to the class, instructing them to analyze the problem and develop options for its resolution. The group was divided into two teams, with the engineers naturally gravitating toward one side of the room and the sales and marketing professionals moving to the opposite side. Jane joined the engineers, "*My people*" as she recalled the event. However, Jane observed something as she sat with the engineers and listened to the discussion about the problem. "*The engineers quickly decided on 'the answer' to the problem; they were very black and white in their thinking.*" Jane said she realized that the engineers were missing other perspectives about the problem. "*They saw the problem in the same way we would see a 'bug' in a computer program; there was one answer to how to fix the problem.*" Jane realized that her passion about her work was in being able to see many sides to a problem. "*I was more comfortable dealing within the shades of gray,*" she said. As a result of this, Jane approached her supervisor about moving to a management path vs. the engineering path that was her predicted future. "*He thought I was crazy. He reminded me that Edgar Codd* (the creator of IBM's relational database technology, DB2) *was my hero.*" Jane was persistent and made a point to network with women to establish relationships in the area she wished to join. Reluctantly, Jane's supervisor supported the move, even helping Jane find her next opportunity within IBM. Jane transitioned to account management, becoming one of the company's first female executives to lead a European market. She credits the ah-ha moment in the seminar as a key turning point in her thinking about what it means to be a leader in the field of technology.

Wait: When I Did Stop Being an Entrepreneur?

Similar to Jane, Bev experienced "an ah-ha moment" during a professional/networking event. A summa cum laude graduate from an Ivy League university with a double major in Political Science and Psychology, Bev's parents pressured her to follow in their footsteps with a career as a tenured university professor. While conducting the research that was intended for her doctoral thesis, Bev realized that there was a business opportunity to consolidate and normalize the sources for the data she was collecting. She drafted a 2-page business plan and approached one of the data providers with her idea to create an industry data exchange.

Convincing her parents that she would abandon the idea after 1 year if it was not successful, Bev left the world of academia, and with the support of a trusted friend (who would later become her husband), launched a software company. Over the next 4 years, the company would grow from a 2-person startup to an international enterprise, with offices in London, San Francisco, and Washington, DC and approximately 45 employees. Bev served as the CEO, growing the business through acquisitions of companies that had potential to become competitors and others that provided complementary services to the core product. Profits were consistently plowed right back into the business and while Bev was rich on paper, she and her family, which now included two children, lived very simply. At the beginning of her fifth year as CEO of this growth business and the exhausting pace of work and constant travel that accompanied it, Bev received a telephone call from a gentleman whose company she had acquired 2 years prior. This time, the caller wanted to buy Bev's company. "*My reaction was immediate,*" Bev recalled. "*I said 'No'.*" Accustomed to being the buyer, not the seller, Bev continued a relentless pace of work and travel, while trying to be a wife and mother for her growing family. Six months later, Bev was invited to serve as a judge for a world-famous competition for entrepreneurs and startup businesses in Aspen, Colorado. Bev recalls that her ah-ha moment occurred when she watched the various entrepreneurs pitch their business ideas. "*The energy they demonstrated was the same energy I used to have about my business before it became all about making payroll, negotiating contracts, worrying about market share and the next competitor.*" Bev flew home from Aspen and spent several weeks talking with her husband, children, parents and with God. Two months after she served as a judge for the entrepreneurial competition, Bev called her attorney. "*I'm ready,*" she said. "*Let's sell the company.*" Bev credits her pivotal moment with allowing her to recognize that her passion is with starting new concepts and new companies, not with serving as a day-to-day, operational leader. In the years that have passed since she sold her company, she has launched a number of enterprises, including a nonprofit that helps to match entrepreneurs who need venture funding with investors who are looking for the next big thing. And she has never stayed with any of the companies more than 2 years.

An Embarrassing Professional Experience

A woman leader, Kristen, who is today the Executive Director of a large foundation shared how a pivotal change in her thinking came when she had her first professional embarrassment. She had returned from an extended trip to Europe where she had not worked but rather had been able to relax and pursue other interests. She returned to the United States refreshed and ready to take on a project that would result in a significant benefit for others and discovered an opportunity to purchase a large parcel of land that included a historic building with a unique railroad switch house. The project was just what she needed and she enthusiastically promoted and marketed the idea to develop a shopping center with a historic railroad museum to others in the community including her parents, brothers, and local citizens. These individuals were persuaded and provided the funding along with a major loan from a local bank.

Unfortunately, an unforeseen recession occurred and caused the proposed shopping center to fail, resulting in major debt for all those involved. The ah-ha moment occurred when she saw the expression on the face of her mother as she heard the news of the financial situation. She knew at that moment that she had been responsible for her parents and other's significant financial loss. The pivotal learning brought about an understanding that her tremendous power in influencing others needed to be informed through extensive research before involving others to lessen the risk of adverse consequences. Kristen has used this learning experience in her career as she has served in many successful capital campaigns serving to raise millions of dollars for various causes and ventures. Today Kristen is on the giving side of the fund raising effort but still uses the ah-ha moment to research carefully those to whom the funding of her current organization benefits before selecting the recipients.

Growing as a CEO

Another pivotal event came to a woman in our interviews, Kassie, from attending a seminar where the theory and practice of situational leadership was taught. She was in her first CEO position and led her organization in a way that many first-time CEOs do in that she made most of the key decisions and solved most of the problems herself. The key staff in the organization would bring the issues to her and she would advise the course of action to take. She was given in the seminar a new way of approaching her leadership style by assessing the competencies and confidence of her staff along with the situation that was faced in order to determine the most effective approach to apply. After the seminar she changed her leadership style and began to empower her staff to make most of the needed decisions or recommendations for them, using their own good judgement. In so doing, she not only had her own change in thinking and behavior in leading others, she also created ah-ha moments for her staff which resulted in pivotal changes for them. She grew as a CEO is her confidence in being a CEO who could delegate (using her time for more strategic initiatives) and her staff also grew in their competencies and confidence.

Learning the Need for Assertiveness

One participant, Josie, reflected upon how early in her career she had been promoted to a position of regional director of human resources, the first woman, serving as a member of an executive team over ten or so hotels in a large hospitality organization. Also serving on the team were other directors of operations, finance, and marketing, all reporting to a regional vice president. All male. The strategic role of human resources was not as prevalent as a practice at the time as it is today so some were not accustomed to human resource professionals contributing in more than a tactical manner such as with tasks for recruitment, hiring, training, policy compliance, and similar. When she realized that strategic planning and budgeting meetings were being held without her being included, she found a way to learn of the meetings and began attending without an invitation. The first time she attended, she was told she did not need to be there but stayed anyway with the excuse that she wanted to learn more about the challenges the hotels faced. She shared that she knew it was her time to assert herself and while it would have been easier to just leave, she had the courage to stay. She continued to attend similar meetings and made suggestions and contributions that were recognized as strategically valuable. Over time the role of the HR professional on the regional teams was changed to be one of a strategic contributor alongside the other directors.

This is an example of creating pivotal learning through our behaviors over time rather than in one ah-ha moment but it was also a learning experience for the woman when she realized she needed to be assertive, demonstrate new behaviors in order for individuals to realize the value the position could bring to the business. She thought they all knew what the role could contribute, but they did not. She said she recalls how she reflected on the first meeting while driving home and also later that evening, thinking she must have been naive to think she, as the first woman in the position, would be accepted as an equal contributor in a strategic role.

The Power of a 360-Degree Assessment

Another woman, Cecilia, is a CEO of a large nonprofit organization who shared how a 360-degree performance appraisal brought her a realization about her leadership competencies and how she exhibited them that changed her way of thinking about allowing conflicts to work themselves out. Feedback from her direct reports and her board of directors provided opinions about the way in which she confronted conflicts about decisions or points of view about possible avenues for growth and the use of the funding received by the organization. The organization is one that provides crucial services to the homeless and others disadvantaged and the need is tremendous with never enough funding to serve all in need. She rated herself low on the element of confronting conflicts and her staff plus the board did the same. She felt by doing so, the staff could come to a better decision if they were left alone to resolve their differences. The ah-ha moment came when the administrator of the 360-degree feedback shared the dichotomy of ratings. The CEO felt that confronting conflict was not important and her staff and her board of directors felt it was very important. She realized for the first time that she needed to intervene more when conflicts arose. She had formerly not intervened or allowed others the opportunity to achieve an effective resolution on their own and felt it was the right approach. She immediately had conversations with all those providing her input to reach an understanding about when and how she would be asked to set in. They decided that a weekly review of pending funding decisions would provide a needed time and place for the discussion and also worked on a structure to evaluate and decide on which project received the funding. A year later when a follow-up 360-degree feedback review was taken, there was significant evidence of change. She also found that funding decisions were shorter and therefore the funding for needed services were quicker, allowing the clients to be served more expeditiously.

Learning to Lead

Ah-ha moments occur for leaders of any age and in all stages of the leadership journey. Joanie is a 30-year-old Director of Content Strategy for the Internet channel of a large organization focused on providing information, products, and services to baby boomers. She leads a team of 15 employees, all of whom are significantly older than Joanie. She admits that leading a team of professionals, many of whom are older than her parents, has come with more than its fair share of ah-ha moments. "*While I may know a lot of about developing content for the Internet, my team knows much more than I do about the subjects that matter to our readers,*" she says. Joanie shared that she approached this position differently than she had in previous jobs. "*I spend a lot more time listening in our team meetings, especially when we are discussing new content ideas and assignments. In the past, I would have made the decision on who would lead the development of a story. But now, I encourage the employees to decide this among themselves.*"

When asked if she has used ah-ha moments with her team, Joanie shared a story about one team member, a woman in her 50s, who delivers *solid* results, but who does not appear to engage effectively with others on the team. "*During my first year as her manager, I made her my project—I spent a lot of time trying to get to know her on both a personal and professional level, coaxing her to talk about her interests, but getting nowhere. I figured she just didn't want to get to know me.*" As time progressed, Joanie started to receive feedback from a number of her team members that this woman was "*difficult to work with.*" They said that their colleague rarely shared important information with other team members and would only provide a status on her content research or development when directly asked. Joanie confirmed that these behaviors were, in fact, occurring on a regular basis and scheduled time to speak with this employee. Providing the employee with this feedback, Joanie was surprised to learn that the employee was *clueless* that her actions were perceived by her colleagues as challenging. "*We discussed how she might go about changing the perceptions of her colleagues.*" Joanie said she noticed that the employee starting to going to lunch at the same time as many of the others in the department and would ask to sit with the others at their table. "*In the past, she always went to run errands on her lunch break or did some other activity alone,*" Joanie shared. During team meetings, Joanie noticed this employee would contribute more, proactively providing status on her work without being asked. "*I knew things had changed when I heard one team member comment that she didn't know what had happened to <this woman>, but whatever it was, she was a much easier to work with.*"

Unfortunately, Joanie's victory was short-lived. The employee soon resigned her position, indicating that she found it exhausting to have to connect so often with her colleagues. In a follow-up conversation with Joanie, she indicated that the result provided an ah-ha moment for her in that she needs to appreciate a broader diversity of working styles and behaviors, especially for good performers.

The Iceberg

Amy is now in her 30s and recalls how in her first leadership role in a male dominated sports organization that she felt, being a young woman working with all men, that she needed to always demonstrate that she was holding her own, being in charge, and was terrified to show any sign of weakness. It was not until one day when she was having her weekly one-on-one session with the person to whom she reported that she realized that she did not need to always handle things by herself without discussing it with others. She came to this new realization when she was told "*you don't have to wait until the boat is sinking (to share the situation with others and ask for advice), it would be better to do so when you see an iceberg.*" She also learned in the same conversation that she did not have to "*be in it all*" to manage the process. This was the first time she felt she had been given permission by herself and others to not always have all the answers or be in total control of situations. She had felt it was a sign of weaknesses and was relieved to learn it was not. It was very freeing to know she did not need to pretend that she knew everything and was on top of everything. She moved on to a major university where she is also still in a male dominated athletic department of the institution and as now the leader of it, she is incorporating her former boss' practice of uninterrupted one-on-one meetings and learning about asking for help with her direct reports.

Graphic 3

Observations on Best Practices of Pivotal Learning Experiences

As witnessed in the stories they shared, each of the women who participated in our interviews for this chapter in the book experienced pivotal changes in their leadership thinking and in many cases, their leadership behavior as a result of taking time to recognize and critically reflect on an ah-ha moment. In each case, the woman had to recognize the occurrence of an ah-ha moment. In many instances, this recognition was not instantaneous, the result of a specific trigger or catalytic event; in fact, the majority of the individuals interviewed indicated that their ah-ha moments were formed over time, often days, weeks, or months after a specific event had occurred.

Of importance is that all of the women interviewed indicated the pivotal learning that led to a significant change in thinking and/or behavior required that they take time for deep reflection. Slowing down to allow oneself time for critical reflection may be viewed as a luxury or an indulgence that few cannot afford, especially in this "24/7 always connected and always doing" world. However, as demonstrated by the interviewees, the act of deliberately slowing down, of taking time to replay the ah-ha moment in one's mind, to pause and reflect, allowed artificial boundaries, behaviors, perceptions, and long-held beliefs to be questioned or dissolved. More importantly, these critical moments of reflection opened the door for new thoughts, assumptions, paradigms, and leadership behaviors to be contemplated and eventually embraced.

The women interviewed also indicated the importance of having a trusted person to dialogue with about their ah-ha moment and its implications on their leadership thinking and behavior. Some women shared their thoughts and experiences with a spouse, a friend, or a colleague. Many used the services of an executive coach who could serve as a truly impartial and yet skilled partner to help analyze the moments and develop a plan of action to implement the desired or necessary changes. Several of those interviewed who engaged an executive coach commented on the value of the coach as an accountability partner—i.e., holding them accountable for what they have said they wish to do to make changes (Rogers, 2008).

From our research and interviews, as well as our own experiences as organizational and business leaders, we offer for your consideration the following best practices for using ah-ha moments as a catalyst for continued learning and leadership momentum:

Hone Your Ah-Ha Moment Intuition

A few of the women leaders interviewed provided examples of a single, sudden experience that served as a pivotal learning moment. One woman shared hearing a news story about a fatal car accident that occurred on the same route she traveled to and from her office every day. The accident occurred at the exact time she would have been driving the route on her evening commute, except she had left work early to attend a recital at her daughter's school—an event she had nearly cancelled due to a looming work deadline. While these jolts or triggers can signal ah-ha moments, we heard the more common experience of a gradual or iterative process that leads to a revelation worthy of critical reflection. Many women leaders talked about recognizing a pattern of thinking or behavior when examining their calendar entries for the previous 6 months or by taking time to read their journal entries from the past year or a favorite blog. It was the ability to see the pattern of thought or behavior that provided the ah-ha moment.

Our research indicates that ah-ha moments that lead to pivotal learning can be the result of both sudden events and analysis of events or thoughts over a longer course of time. Ah-ha moments can manifest themselves through many formats, from doing an activity, reading a story, or receiving feedback from another person. A best practice that was revealed through the interviews is to honor your intuition on the activities, thoughts, and information that can lead to an ah-ha moment. If we can be more acutely aware of what is occurring around us and recognize the events, feelings, and signs that have the potential to become ah-ha moments, we will have the opportunity to embrace the learning that can result from this pivotal change.

Practice Quiet Time

The importance of allowing time for critical reflection cannot be overstated as a key component of transformative learning. Many of the women leaders we interviewed incorporate time into their schedules to simply quiet their minds. Some of the women regularly practice yoga or meditation as a means of finding the quiet time they need for reflection. Others mentioned starting each day with 10 or 15 min to contemplate the previous day's (or week's) events. Others found their quiet time in prayer or in keeping a gratitude journal. Reviewing the journal as a reflection proved to be helpful in revealing patterns to thoughts and feedback from others, resulting in ah-ha moments.

The practice of being still provides the avenue to listen to the inner voices that allow the reflection process to start. Executive coaches often use this concept of holding the space with their clients—i.e., maintaining silence as a means of encouraging deeper thought and critical reflection.

What is clear from the research and the interviews is that we can train ourselves to recognize ah-ha moments and that they are more likely to reveal themselves when we allow ourselves to be still and clear our minds of unnecessary clutter.

Find Your Wing (Wo)man

A key component of pivotal learning is having meaningful dialogue with another person, an individual who you respect to provide complete and unbridled honesty and who will maintain confidentiality of the conversation. While spouses and best friends were cited by some of the women interviewed, a majority of them mentioned using the services of an executive coach to help facilitate the focused learning process. Engaging the services of a executive coach to support the pivotal learning process can be effective as coaches are change agents trained to motivate and support individuals with new hope, purpose, and concrete actions for sustaining positive leadership behaviors and thoughts (Hudson, 1999). And unlike a spouse, sibling, or friend, an executive coach comes to the relationship with no agenda other than to work with clients to achieve efficient, increased and sustainable effectiveness in their lives and careers through focused learning (Rogers, 2008).

Options Abound for Finding This Ally, Your Wing (Wo)man

The best practice to note is that having honest and meaningful discourse with an individual who will be completely candid and open to sharing their perspectives is an essential component of converting the ah-ha moment to a pivotal learning opportunity.

Plan to Act and Act to Plan

The final best practice from our research is to develop an action plan for implementing the changes in the leadership thinking and behaviors you wish to undertake. Virtually all of the women interviewed noted that as a result of their critical reflection of the ah-ha moment and the dialogue about the moment with a trusted resource, they developed a plan that outlined steps to support the changes they desired. Some women developed written plans as a measure of accountability; others mentioned that their plans were mental notes or emotional commitments, in essence promises made to oneself to embrace different leadership thinking or behaviors. Regardless of whether the plan is a structured, written document or a mental checklist, the commitment to planning to act or think differently is the common best practice among the women we interviewed.

Graphic 4

Conclusion

Leaders are responsible for learning (Senge, 1990). The opportunity for pivotal learning often begins with a realization that our existing leadership beliefs or behaviors need to be assessed in light of new information. This information can reveal itself as a sudden event or intellectual trigger or more gradually over time as an amalgam of thoughts that urge us to commence some inner examination.

As evidenced by the stories they shared, the women who participated in our interviews for this chapter experienced ah-ha moments that opened the door for critical reflection on their thoughts or behaviors. This led to dialogue with a trusted resource and the development of a plan of action, outlining changes that helped to transform their role as leader. Some even used ah-ha moments as an opportunity to foster pivotal learning for others. All reinforced the concept that transformational learning requires recognition of the pivotal moment and a desire to follow a process such as outlined in this chapter. Our hope for each of our readers (and ourselves) is that we will give ourselves the time we require in order to focus on ourselves, to embrace who we are as dynamic and effective leaders and how we can be our own best self.

Graphic 5

References

Bernard, H. R. (1988). *Research methods in cultural anthropology*. Newbury Park, CA: Sage.

Feslinger, L. (1957). *A theory of cognitive dissonance*. Redwood City, CA: Stanford University Press.

Henderson J. (2001). *Transformative learning in the executive suite: CEOs and the role of Context in Mezirow's theory*. Doctoral dissertation, The George Washington University, Washington, DC.

Hudson, F. (1999). *The adult years: Mastering the art of self-renewal*. San Francisco, CA: John Wiley & Sons.

Marshall, J. (2015). *Digital media consumption is booming as investment floods*. Retrieved August 1, 2017, from http://blogs.wsj.com/cmo/2015/08/19/digital-media-consumption-is-booming-as-investment-floods-in/.

Mezirow, J. (1991). *Transformative dimensions of adult learning*. San Francisco, CA: Jossey-Bass.

Mezirow, J. (2011). *Fostering critical reflection in adulthood: A guide to transformative and emancipatory learning 'How critical reflection triggers transformative learning*. San Francisco, CA: Jossey Bass.

Rogers, J. (2008). *Coaching skills*. New York, NY: McGraw-Hill Open University Press.

Senge, P. (1990). *The fifth discipline: The art and practice of the learning organization*. New York, NY: Doubleday.

Turkler, S. (2008). *Ted Talks: Connected, but alone?* Retrieved August 1, 2017, from https://www.ted.com/talks/sherry_turkle_alone_together?language=en.

Reflections of a Woman Airline Pilot

Diane L. Rothberg, Bryan T. Baldwin, and Frank Wilkerson

True leaders understand that leadership is not about them but about those they serve. It is not about exalting themselves but about lifting others up.

Sheri L. Dew

When I close my eyes, I can still fill the surge of power as I advance the throttles. To have been in command of a passenger jet was a privilege and a joy. But it was about far more than those big, beautiful machines. It was also about my journey to leadership, and the people who helped me along the way. Whether in the flight deck, the cabin or on the ground, the folks I worked with during my 25 year airline career were the most talented, convivial, and definitely the most tolerant imaginable.

As the seventh woman to be hired by the airline in 1985, I was promoted to Captain in 1998, one of a handful of women to earn the responsibility of command. Women in many "male-dominated" professions have also become leaders, but many have not, and the question is, why not? After all, for years now, women have had the freedom to select any university, any profession, and any lifestyle they desire. But, after buckets of money spent, and a bellyful of affirmative action programs, the number of women in a leadership role, particularly in technical professions, remains surprisingly small.

D. L. Rothberg (✉)
Gainesville, GA, USA

B. T. Baldwin · F. Wilkerson
Cumming, GA, USA

F. L. Denmark, M. A. Paludi (eds.), *Women and Leadership*,
https://doi.org/10.1007/978-3-319-72182-8_2

Hiring the First Women

When my airline made the decision to hire women, it was probably not an easy one. Pilots are a traditional bunch, many from a military or an engineering background. The corporation had to have been concerned not only about our ability to do the job, but also about how 2000 male pilots might feel about having us "force-fed" into their culture. In the airlines, safety must always be paramount, and even the most open-minded person can be forgiven for feeling that 37,000 ft may not be the best place for social experimentation. One thing our airline management did right was to ensure they applied the exact same hiring criteria to the women as to the men. Indeed, most all of the women they hired on those first courses far exceeded the minimum qualifications. This was, in part, because many of them who had been declined by the airlines over the years still remained active in the industry, gaining experience and accumulating even more flight time.

We were hired two at a time, so that over our 3 month initial training period, we would have the companionship and understanding of someone of our own gender should we need it. And we did. The initial course was no joke. Even after 10 years in aviation, I found I needed to spend every waking moment studying. There was lots of new information to absorb on jet engines and high level meteorology, plus a myriad of rules, regulations, and company procedures. And all this was before we were even assigned our aircraft! I became good friends with the only other woman, and also with the guys on the course. We were all young, loved aviation, and were hugely excited about starting our airline careers. We took to studying together, eating together, and fretting before the exams together.

Exam performance was absolutely crucial, particularly because it formed the basis for the assignment of our seniority numbers. Seniority completely governs career advancement and quality of life in the airline industry, and its importance cannot be overstated. I ended up about halfway down the list, and I can't count the number of times I missed out on a promotion, or a new aircraft because I was just a few numbers too junior. I would often have to wait months or even years for the next opportunity to move up. We all managed to pass the initial course, and the two women who walked into the classroom as oddities, walked out as part of a tight little group of a dozen brand-new pilot applicants, all of whom started on the same level playing field and shared the same initiation experience. Indeed, the friendships we made in that classroom lasted throughout our entire careers.

Integration into the Larger Peer Group

After completing 6 weeks of simulator training and the required check flights, I qualified as a Second Officer (Flight Engineer) on a B-727. This was actually a nonflying position. As the third crew member, the Second Officer sat sideways on the flight deck and monitored such systems as fuel, electrics, hydraulics, and pressurization. Although third in command on the flight deck, this position was considered the "lowest of the low."

I was assigned to one of the smallest company bases, and the arrival of their first woman pilot was a bigger deal than I ever expected. When I walked into the flight planning area on my first day, the entire room stopped to stare at the astonishing sight of a navy-blue uniform with bumps in all the wrong places. Initially, the men were cordial but wary, sniffing around me like dogs at a hydrant. But I was fortunate in that I worked with professionals who cared about one thing, and one thing only, and that was my competency.

In the flying business, a pilot's skill level is on display long before you even board the aircraft. The Captain will know from your initial assessment of the flight plan, whether you have taken the time to study it thoroughly. He will see right away if you have a good understanding of weather, of fuel management, and if you can correctly deal with maintenance issues that may allow you to fly but limit you operationally.

If you take your job seriously and work hard at it, you will surely gain the respect of your fellow crew members. And, once they respect you, if you are a decent enough human being, they might even start to like you. It can be astonishing to watch the prejudices slip away. Once you get into the swing of reading the checklists and start dealing with the business of the flight, the novelty of your presence quickly wears off. There is nothing like an "eventful" flight, perhaps bad weather, a medical emergency, or a bomb scare, to transcend any differences in personality or gender.

The Example of "Command"

The Second Officer seat was a great vantage point from which to observe the Captain, whose leadership style always set the tone in the cockpit. I always preferred working with those Captains who really knew the airplane and their jobs. They tended to have a quiet confidence about them, were never "blowhards," and were great mentors and instructors. One of my most unforgettable lessons in leadership occurred one stormy night on the East Coast.

The Captain was flying the approach in turbulence and a strong crosswind. It was the task of the First Officer and myself to closely monitor his altitude, airspeed, and descent rate, and to call out any deviations. Well, the landing was a real thumper, not enough to damage the aircraft, but enough to give the passengers something to talk about. The Captain was silent as he exited the runway. He set the parking brake, turned to us and said, "I'm so sorry. I'm not exactly sure what went wrong there, but tell me everything you saw." I will never forget the humility and honesty of that captain, and I immediately decided that his was the sort of example I wanted to follow.

But it wasn't always so easy, and on one particular check ride, I got a rude "wake up call."

In those days, we underwent four flight checks a year in a full motion simulator, where a crew could experience those rare emergencies that are too dangerous to practice in the real aircraft. Engine failures, fires, hydraulic problems, and electrical failures were always on the menu, and the actions of the crew were assessed by a Check Pilot who observed from the back. We were knee deep in a particularly complex hydraulic problem which involved the Second Officer cranking the landing gear down manually. This action was to occur late in the approach when a safe landing was assured, since once the gear was down, it couldn't be raised again, thus eliminating the option of an overshoot. Well, I got impatient, didn't wait for the command, and started cranking the gear down too early.

During the post-flight debriefing, I insisted that I thought I heard the Captain call for the gear. Nothing much was said, but later on, when I happened to be following the Captain and the Check Pilot down the hallway, I overheard the Check Pilot saying. "I can't stand when someone makes excuses." The comment disturbed me for days, and I was forced to take a good, hard look at myself, and my professional conduct. I swore, then and there, that I would always be completely honest with my fellow crew members. It was a leadership lesson I tried never to forget.

Promotion to First Officer

It is unlikely that any career offers a fairer opportunity for promotion than that of an Airline Pilot. Your seniority number is inviolate, and you cannot be passed over, no matter your race, color, gender, or popularity with management. But this "equal opportunity" coin has two sides. You are offered an "opportunity" for promotion, but there is no guarantee of success. You must take the course, meet the standards, and pass rigorous testing. After more than 3 years as a Second Officer, I'll never forget that phone call informing me that I was slotted for training as a First Officer on the DC-9. I was ecstatic! I would no longer be sitting sideways, and I would soon have my own set of flight controls!

The DC-9 had the reputation of being a beautiful bird to fly. Being an older and less automated aircraft, it required good, old-fashioned flying skills, and its pilots were respected as having good "hands and feet." I couldn't wait to get my hands on it. The transition to this new aircraft took well over a month of ground school, simulator, and flight training. It was very intense, with one instructor assigned to each pair of pilots, ideally one Captain and one First Officer. This was a two crew aircraft and required no Second Officer.

I was fortunate to be assigned a wonderful instructor and a good training partner. As a woman, I don't think I was ever treated any differently than the men. I was tested thoroughly, but never given any additional "tricks" to try and humiliate me. The instructors and examiners were always helpful and supportive, but I must say, I always found these transition courses to be hugely difficult and challenging. I wasn't the only applicant who found it worthwhile to pay for a hotel room, so I could devote every extra moment to study, without any of the distractions of home life.

It was as a First Officer that I felt fully apprenticed to the job of Captain. The First Officer's job was, on the face of it, not that much different than the Captain's. You normally alternated flight legs, and when you were not flying, you worked the radios, navigated and managed the aircraft systems. But there was never any doubt as to who had the final word, and who bore the ultimate responsibility for the safe outcome of the flight. In fact, in certain marginal weather conditions, the First Officer was not even permitted to fly the approach. A good Captain, however, would empower you to exercise your decision-making skills, particularly when you were at the flight controls. I came to appreciate that there was much more to the Captain's job than meets the eye. It takes knowledge, experience, and a cool head to make complex, critical, and timely decisions, particularly if your "office" happens to be buffeting in turbulence, or is on fire. There were certain situations where I found I was quite grateful to defer to the Captain, and I suddenly understood why he was earning so much more money than I.

After a time as First Officer, one of your regular flight checks would be designated as a "Captain's Potential Assessment." It really wasn't much different from any other flight check, except your decision-making skills were evaluated more closely. An early assessment of command skills gave the company the ability to deal with potential problems early. Not very many pilots did poorly on these assessments, since the airline was proud of its efforts to "hire Captains from day one." But there were a few who were encouraged not to seek promotion. My next career move was also a First Officer position, but on a B-767. A large, modern, long-range machine, it gave me the opportunity to transition to a sophisticated cockpit with the latest technological developments and also to experience overseas flying.

As the years went by, I worked hard to hone not only my piloting skills, but also my diplomatic skills. Teamwork is everything, but there is a delicate balance to be maintained. While it is important to be respectful and deferential to the Captain, you must have the confidence and skill to assert yourself should you feel the safety of the operation is at stake. There are many accident reports that describe in tragic detail what can happen when the First Officer does not do so.

Promotion to Captain

Whenever a new aircraft assignment is posted, the pilots cluster around it, anxious to see the results of their bids. When I finally pushed through the crowd and saw my name on the Captain's list, I could barely believe it, especially since it was to be on my beloved DC-9. But as my course date grew closer, I grew more and more nervous. The Captain's course at our airline was extremely rigorous, and not everyone passed. What was worse, if you failed it, you did not necessarily have the option to go back to your old position. You could be out the door. When I confided my concerns to some of the more seasoned Captains, they assured me that my fears were normal. They admitted that they too had experienced them, and furthermore, any First Officer who didn't feel self-doubt was probably not ready for promotion.

After so many years in a supporting role, it was now my turn for the spotlight. It would be my name that would be listed on the flight plan, and I would be the one called into the office should anything go awry on my flight. The aircraft course was much easier this time, because I had already flown the DC-9 as a First Officer. But it's amazing how different the world can be from the left-hand side of the cockpit. For one thing, that's the side the nose wheel steering is on. For the first time, I would be required to taxi the aircraft, and would have to find my way around huge airports such as Chicago, Atlanta, and New York. I truly did fear getting lost, and the expression "woman driver" came to mind more than once.

At this point in his career, the Captain's flying ability is presumed. What he really needs to demonstrate is the ability to "manage." And it's astonishing, the array of resources that must be managed for even one short flight. Firstly, there are the human resources. In a large airline, the Captain might well be meeting his First Officer and the Flight Attendants for the very first time. He must quickly establish a relaxed atmosphere and open lines of communication, but leave no doubt that everyone's job must be performed correctly and efficiently. He must do the same in his dealings with maintenance, flight dispatch, ground crews and anyone else associated with the flight. Then, there are the technical resources. These pertain to the safe operation of the flight. While a "suggested" flight plan is provided by company dispatch, the Captain is responsible for carefully analyzing the weather and flight conditions, and making amendments to the routing, altitude, alternate airport, or additional fuel as he sees fit. Fuel is one of the most important resources a Captain must manage, since it is expensive to carry, but priceless if needed.

Once aboard the aircraft, the Captain must manage a moving office in an atmosphere of ever-changing conditions. To ensure that the job is done in an orderly fashion every time, and that nothing is forgotten, checklists are used for pretty much everything. A huge part of the Captain's training is the proper use of these checklists. Normal Checklists quickly become a matter of rote, but when something goes wrong, properly integrating them into the Emergency Drills and Emergency Checklists becomes vital. Much time is spent in the simulator learning how to do this. I enthusiastically applied myself to the ground school and simulator phases of the course, but thoroughly dreaded the next step, the "Command Simulators." Ours was one of the few airlines that required these two additional simulator sessions for their Captain candidates.

The aim of these sessions was to determine, once and for all, if you really had the "right stuff," before the company handed you a multimillion dollar asset filled with over a hundred people, some of whom might be their family members. The idea was to overload you with multiple failures and then assess your ability to organize, prioritize, coordinate your crew, and make logical decisions under intense stress. They wanted to make sure that if your airplane was flying on one engine, low on fuel and filling with smoke, you could get the thing on the ground, even if you didn't have the luxury or time to complete all the checks.

Passing those Command Simulators was a huge relief, and a great confidence booster. Now I could really enjoy the rest of the course, which entailed actually getting out and flying the airplane. All new Captains were required to fly their first 50 h with a fully qualified Captain serving as their First Officer. This way, we could get the feel of the job, but still have someone there to provide the benefit of their experience. It was during this 50 h period that I was suddenly reminded of my gender. The first few times I arrived on board the aircraft to brief the Flight Attendants, many were aghast at the sight of a female Captain. However, most were absolutely delighted, and showed their love by making sure I got the best leftover food from the back.

Finally, the official day of my promotion came. It was customary to receive your Captain's wings in an unusual and interesting way, and mine came in the middle of a flight, hidden on my breakfast tray under a linen napkin. When I walked into flight planning for the first time as a fully qualified Captain, the reaction was so much different than on that day so many years ago when I first joined the airline. When my fellow pilots spotted my fourth stripe, they immediately swarmed me, pumped my hand and there were hugs all around.

It took a while for me to get used to having my very own First Officer. It was now me who was being deferred to and looked to for approval. There was very little in the way of gender issues however, because these men were professionals, knew what it took to become a Captain and respected the position. Of course, everything was not always rosy, and as a person with a strong personality, I got along with some people better than others. But it was a great epiphany for me to realize that people could dislike me for all sorts of reasons, the least of which was my gender.

As the years went by the airline hired more women, and several became my First Officers. Flying with them was really no different than flying with the guys. But it sure could be fun watching the expressions on the passengers' faces when they realized that they were in the hands of not just one woman pilot, but two!

Like all Captains I was required to cope with countless challenges, most weather-related, in the form of thunderstorms, rain, fog, turbulence, crosswinds, snow, and ice. There were also mechanical problems, medical emergencies, bomb scares, passenger issues, and more. I was also faced with several serious in-flight emergencies. One was an engine failure at high altitude due to an oil leak. We landed safely at an en route airport. Another was an engine failure late in the takeoff roll. I needed to apply aggressive braking and reverse to stop the aircraft on the remainder of the runway. The brakes completely melted, we were unable to move, and flights were thoroughly disrupted at that airport for several hours. It was thanks to good training and excellent crew support that these stories had happy endings.

After several delightful years on the DC-9, I moved up to Captain on the Airbus A-320, a highly automated, larger, and more modern aircraft. I flew to most major cities in North America, and became senior enough to be able to pick and choose my flights, and even get Christmas off! But with seniority comes age, and it is from this aircraft that I eventually retired. My 25 year airline career seemed to pass in the blink of an eye, and I am left with so many warm and wonderful memories not the least of which was the privilege of having been accepted into the "band of brothers," my wonderful, fellow pilots. I had such a great time. No two flights were ever the same, and each day held a new adventure. I was treated fairly, had the identical advancement opportunities as the men, earned a good salary, and got to see the world.

So, the question remains, why do so many women choose to overlook this wonderful profession? Sure, I was away from home a lot and had to work plenty of nights, weekends, and holidays. But so did the Flight Attendants and women were not dissuaded from pursuing that career. I have my theories on this, but I can't really answer that question. Now that you have read my story, can you?

Becoming a Leader

Florence L. Denmark, Krystal Lozada, and Jennifer Ledesma

> *Although we weren't able to shatter that highest, hardest glass ceiling this time, thanks to you, it's got about 18 million cracks in it...You can be so proud that, from now on, it will be unremarkable for a woman to win primary state victories... unremarkable to have a woman in a close race to be our nominee, unremarkable to think that a woman can be the president of the United States. And that is truly remarkable, my friends.*
>
> Hillary Clinton

Becoming a leader must start with the individual's desire to seize opportunities so to best develop his/her skills. However, striving to be a leader does not mean that an individual of 15–20 years old has to build a nonprofit company from the ground up or come up with an idea to transform social injustices. Becoming a leader can begin with something as small as getting involved in an organization of interest or seeking leadership possibilities within professional job settings. The goal of an individual striving for a leadership position must first find and grow his/her passions, confidence, and skill sets to become a trailblazer.

In order to best understand how to become a leader, it is important to define the term, "leader." This term has never had a straightforward single definition; it varies with circumstances since the emergence of leaders is often situational, sometimes temporary or sometimes permanent. Many have attempted to clarify the concept of leadership. Goleman defined the leader as someone that has marked intelligence or someone who along with a high IQ and technical skills possesses a high level of emotional intelligence (Goleman, 1998). The concept of emotional intelligence was

F. L. Denmark (✉)
Department of Psychology, Pace University, New York, NY, USA
e-mail: fdenmark@pace.edu

K. Lozada · J. Ledesma
Pace University, New York, NY, USA

F. L. Denmark, M. A. Paludi (eds.), *Women and Leadership*,
https://doi.org/10.1007/978-3-319-72182-8_3

viewed as important for leadership and has been interpreted through "The Five components of Emotional Intelligence at Work" which are self-regulation, self-awareness, internal motivation, empathy, and social skills (Goleman, 1998). As a young person, who is developing and making conscious decisions, it is important to understand that emotional intelligence is something that can only increase with age and experience. It is also important to know that the potentiality of leadership is an ongoing process. Individuals need to grasp that a leader is not born with the skill sets to flourish; rather it is hard work, dedication, and passion that pushes them forward to become successful.

One should know that leaders are not restricted to a specific race, gender, age, or ethnicity, but that leadership is a continuation composed of emotional intelligence, standard smarts, personal experiences, values, beliefs, and motivation to help make a change (Denmark, 1977). Additional definitions focus on several components central to leadership, including viewing leadership as a process involving influence, occurring within a group context and involving a goal to be attained (Rowe, 2007). The aforementioned attempts at defining a leader all are true, but to further simplify what is a leader; it can refer to any individual who helps a group meet their goals. Thus, a leader has a clear influence within the group, yet does not necessarily have to be the nominal leader. That individual can also demonstrate leadership qualities in various situations such as making a joke that alleviates group tension or someone who offers to help in a time of crisis. In today's society, the skills and behaviors needed to be a successful leader are learned and not innate (Rowe, 2007). Thus, there are varying ways in which an individual can become a leader or reach leadership potential.

Mentor Relationships

The literature surrounding mentored relationships has varied but generally has encouraged the impact that a mentor can have on an individual. Some research has focused on the psychosocial and career aspects of a mentored relationship. In a psychosocial relationship, the mentor serves as a counselor, friend, advocate, and role model to the mentee but in terms of career, the mentor helps in coaching and sponsoring the mentee in networking (Mayer, Files, Ko, & Blair, 2008). Through the process of networking, it may also be possible to find a mentor. Mentorship has been associated with great advantages to those rising in leadership. Traditional mentor systems follow a dyadic model where a more experienced individual is joined with a less experienced individual. Experienced mentors can offer support and collaboration to newer individuals that will build their esteem and practical value. They can also offer the mentee an opportunity to work with them on various ongoing projects, thus increasing that individual's skill level and competence. Mentors may desire to mold and guide the next generation of leaders and shared values and interest may bring two people together for this relationship. This relationship may eventually foster independence in a rising leader. Mentored relationships have been identified as having positive impacts on improved educational outcomes varying from jobs to academic success. In multiple mentoring models, a mentee is encouraged to construct a community of mentors that can support them along their career path. Each mentor can address and support different aspects of a career and together it would be more likely to obtain a comprehensive view as well as offer a broader range of psychosocial support. This network of support seems ideal in that it allows for a wide array of mentorship experiences.

A study conducted by John P. Dugan and Susan R. Komives that was representative of 50 colleges across 25 states in 2010, found that meaningful relationships between students and faculty can impact outcomes related to socially responsible leadership. They also found that peer interactions contributed to that outcome as well. As individuals across cultures spoke of different lifestyles, social issues, or their own personal values, it had a positive impact on the role of leadership that peers can offer. The path in becoming a socially responsible leader is difficult, but this study proved that mentored relationships could in fact add to a student's leadership skill set so she/he can better solve social problems in an ethical and responsible way.

Peer-mentoring models have also shown positive effects on the experience of rising leadership through community encouragement and increased sense of group affiliation (Mayer et al., 2008). The support of a peer network seems fundamental in being able to climb the leadership ladder. Peer groups may actually de-emphasize hierarchy and seniority. Instead, peer groups are a great way of providing mutual support and learning, engaging with different perspectives, and developing important relationships with individuals in the same field and of similar rank. The disadvantage in peer groups is not having a more experienced member of the field to guide and foster leadership skills.

In most schools across America, the use of academic advisors as acting mentors has been found useful in engaging students with their school atmospheres. This is perhaps the easiest way a student can attain a mentor, but students can also look for mentors in someone other than a faculty member. As previously mentioned, young individuals can also look for mentors in other areas such as peers that have more experience in similar but different interests from their own. Given varying opportunities can help the individual explore his/her passions and understand what it takes to become a leader.

Female Constraints

The impacts of societal constraints have been found to have a negative impact on the leadership potential of women. These steady stereotypes and cultural constraints create a certain limitation or as some would say a "glass ceiling," where the female can only reach a certain point before they are forced to ultimately stop. An article written by Alice Eagly and Linda Carli recognized this limitation, but stated that females have a certain advantage in regard to their leadership style under certain contemporary conditions that are essential to the workplace growth. Although research has determined this finding, the competence of the female leader is consistently undermined, especially within masculine organizational contexts, in which a male is still seen as superior over a female (Eagly & Carli, 2003). It is also essential to note that this socialization has been embedded into the minds of young children specifically girls, such escalation does less to promote their leadership capabilities within the workplace, but instead prepares them for the domestic roles as a wife, mothers, or employees of a low level traditional jobs within the workplace (Denmark, 1993). Although there are restraints in being a female leader in a predominately male driven world, both female and male students can equally focus on independent passions of theirs to grow.

It is important that females recognize that they are equally capable of taking on leadership roles when being compared to their male counterparts. This has to do with the confidence in themselves and their potential capabilities. Males have society to encourage them; thus, females need to actively search for outlets where they can shine as leaders. In joining groups, it is essential that young females speak up about their beliefs and encourage others to do so as well. In doing so, it will increase their ability to take control while also maintaining their own views. In a nationwide, qualitative study conducted by the Girl Scouts of the USA in 2007, questioning 4000 boys and girls, between ages 8 and 17, as well as mothers on issues related to leadership. They focused on the girls' definition of leadership, experience of leadership, aspirations, barriers to leadership, the qualities and the skills girls associate with leadership, predictors of leadership, issues related to gender bias and leadership and leadership education and support systems (Schoenberg, Salmond, & Fleshman, 2008, p. 6). The important concept to take note is, the researchers of this study wanted to understand how the girls themselves thought of their potential to become leaders. Their findings alluded to the problem girls face as they seemed to be aware of the gender biases evident in society. The girls in this study reported having lower levels of self-perceptions when compared to the boys in the study and struggled with the "stress, fear of talking in front of others, seeming bossy, and peer pressure" (Schoenberg et al., 2008, p. 7). This study provided more insight into how a female student can cope with the issues they face in becoming a leader and look for ways to rectify this. The girls themselves noted that having successful leadership programs available to them would be beneficial to them, so they can address these inner conflicts and learn to better cope with their problems and develop their leadership skills. They also believed that their environment served to foster their self-confidence and provide a support system (Schoenberg et al., 2008). The effect of gender on leadership capabilities evidently has a clear impact on young females at an early age yet in recognizing these disadvantages; individuals can focus on ways to transform potential setbacks.

The consequence of gender and leadership experiences also has an impact on a female leader's self-efficacy. A study conducted by a Research-I institution in the Midwest wanted to assess the self-efficacy of students based on their prior leadership experiences, gender, and their interpretations of academic support. Students that were active in a campus student organization were measured based on a version of the Student Leadership Practices Inventory. The researchers found that the student leaders used in the study had high self-efficacy according to leadership practices (Bardou, Byrne, Pasternak, Perez, & Rainey, 2003; Posner, 2004). However, they found that females reported higher levels of leadership development when they had direct support of a faculty advisor as opposed to the male students who felt an overall positive support from their institution and leadership development programs (Bardou et al., 2003). This refers back to the concept of the faculty and student mentor relationship essential for their growth of leadership skills.

Girls should concentrate on these issues and join groups that focus on building self-confidence, or interact with other females or faculty members that have successfully achieved leadership roles. Additionally, they should be more active in speaking up in classrooms or saying what's on their mind in small group settings. If there are troubles when speaking in front of people, it's important that these girls face this head-on and join clubs targeted for these problems. There are clubs such as the debate-team or magazine club that can help someone too shy of expressing themselves gain qualities to improve their self-evaluations.

As a young individual, one may ask how can I become a leader if my parents require me to return home directly after school, or if I am a college student and leadership skills are becoming particularly harder to attain? It's important to understand that leaders vary from different styles to different situations and can exert influence in numerous ways (Denmark, 1977). A study conducted by consisted of undergraduate students in which they were presented with a single picture of a business meeting occurring around a table. The results indicated that the students assumed that the person at the head of the table was the leader. However, something also worth noting was that when the picture had a mixed group, consisting of both male and females and a female was seated at the head of the table, most students didn't immediately think of them as a leader. Their results helped to understand two things, the first was that students might simply have to sit at the end of a table to simply appear like a leader and others will view them as such. Secondly, although this study was conducted over 20 years ago, it still points out the problem female leaders are faced with.

Passion

High school or college is the place where individuals tend to find themselves and discover their passions. The passion can grow from involvement in an after-school job, internships, clubs, teams, or subjects; once something has sparked an interest, leadership skills automatically begin to form. The student will begin to form better communication skills as they are constantly communicating with peers and faculty, which will motivate one to help others.

To have commitments and enthusiasm for a specific subject, group, sports team, or job can certainly help form a leader. The important indicator of becoming a leader is having the willingness to seek out passions and create something from them. It's essential for a leader to not only have an education and experience, but also for the individual to be engaged in goal directed activities. In the article, "A Life Skills Development Program for High School Student-Athletes," researchers identified that sports and extracurricular activities serve as the base for the development of self-efficacy. Researchers have also found that sports influence personal development and help to promote essential skills evident in successful leaders. This article highlights the importance of sport participation as a way to help youth develop essential life skills. In doing so, an individual passionate about sports can also use the life skills learned through this activity to develop other leadership skills. Individuals with an interest in either football, baseball, basketball, or track must commit time to learning the sport and focus on ways to enhance their abilities. These are the same qualities needed when an individual moves into a certain profession. They must convert their abilities as young athletes and transform them into an aptitude so they can best perform in a job setting. The stress of balancing work, school, and extracurricular activities can be grueling and difficult; however, time management is essential for a leader. Therefore, through being an athlete, individuals gain experience in time management skills, self-evaluations skills, and the ability to cope and grow with constructive criticisms.

The passion athletes hold can also influence their capability in becoming a leader, especially in how they express themselves. In a study conducted by Mckenna and in which they examined their participants' reactions to a pair of actors ranging from same sex to cross sex who communicated nonverbally. Their results found that regardless of gender, those that exhibited greater nonverbal behavior such as maintaining eye contact or acting more relaxed were perceived to be in a leadership role. Yet more recent studies found that women who expressed anger within a professional context are seen negatively and within a lower status. However, males exhibiting the same behavior are seen as more powerful and higher in status. Although this distinction provides another challenge for young females to face, it also gives them the opportunity to adopt certain styles of communication in an effort to cope with cultural biases and become a leader.

Confidence

The concept of confidence is yet another essential key to attempt at being a leader. The young individual has to be willing to take on risks and be assured that the mistakes they will make will only help them grow. Additionally, there has to be a balance between the individual's self-assurance and their ability to accept criticisms. They must understand that leaders must have these skills in order to thrive in both academic and professional settings. It's also important that the potential leaders have confidence in themselves. If they do not believe in what they are doing or what they are working towards, then they will not gain a following and will be unable to lead or succeed. An individual must exert some influence over others (Denmark, 1993). This could mean the individual is the head of a group project, the speaker of a presentation in a classroom, captain of the soccer team, president of Model UN, or head intern of a law firm. When individuals are confident in themselves and their capabilities, the passion that they hold is evident and makes them better leaders.

The impact of media is also a large influence on the one's self-confidence. It can either inhibit or promote an individual's plan of action on whether they decide to take on leadership roles. This is due in part to the role that many celebrities or politicians hold as exemplar's. Individuals who are highly regarded promote potential passions and leadership qualities that youths are yearning to develop. The most effective method to increase the confidence of potential leaders is to gain experience. These experiences can vary from participating in student council events, to helping the advisor organize the events and finally becoming a student council representative that creates events for the student body to participate in. Further experiences can derive from an internship, job, or volunteering at community events. This will then make their goals and desires as something attainable. The experience the student attains will result in not only an increase in their personal self-confidence but the individual will also gain a reputation as someone that is reputable and knowledgeable. The various roles the individuals can partake in help to grow their attainment as a leader. Through each club, extracurricular, organization that the individual participates in, transferrable leadership skills are also gained.

Leadership Qualities

The misconception that a leader must impact the lives of their peers or community often discourages others of their belief in themselves. However, it's important for young individuals to learn the importance of engaging in the very qualities that makes a great leader, such as open communication to peers, delegation to other members of their group, encouragement, and open-mindedness to other's opinions and beliefs. To be valued as a good leader, it's important that potential leaders don't engage in negative behaviors and are perceived as having a positive outlook. When searching for leadership positions, it's imperative that the individual presents oneself as an optimistic person who is willing to help others, reassure others, and create environments that are representative of many in a group rather than a select few. A leader supports the voices of others and devises ways to have their individual voice be a composition of their followers.

In addition to seeking out ways to enhance leadership capabilities, Barry Posner proposed a leadership development instrument for students to implement in colleges. In various research, it has been identified that the environment in which the student learns is an instrumental factor in how a student can become a leader. This chapter updates the previous Student Leadership Practices Inventory used in the leadership developmental programs that have been implemented in various colleges, nationwide. This inventory that was designed by Posner and colleagues "identifies specific behaviors and actions that students report using when they are at their personal best" which uses the five leadership practices: Modeling the Way, Inspiring a Shared Vision, Challenging the Process, Enabling Others to Act, and

Encouraging the Heart to identify practices common of successful leaders (Posner, 2004). The validity of these measures was found consistent amongst fraternities, sororities, and presidents of other student organizations in which student leaders conveyed those five leadership practices more frequently than their peers. The interesting aspect of this revised inventory is the inclusion of self-efficacy as an important aspect of leadership behavior that many successful leaders practice. The Student Leadership Development Inventory places importance on campus leadership and the positive impact that leadership developmental programs can have over time on a student self-regard and leadership capabilities. This Inventory also emphasized the impact of a student's involvement in extracurricular activities as an important aspect of growth as a leader.

Additionally, a leader must also recognize that they must have followers that are responsive and devoted to them so they will remain in that designated leadership role. If a young leader is not fulfilling their duty for example as a student council representative, then they will be replaced by someone else. A leader of a group should expect to fulfill certain tasks in order to maintain support from their followers and present themselves as someone capable of taking on specific roles. Stresses that the role of a leader is not permanent and is easily interchangeable therefore the individual "must be aware of the responsiveness of their followers—their needs, expectations, and perceptions." This is essential for aspiring leaders to understand that leadership quality must encompass not only their individual skill sets but also the responsiveness of their followers.

Ultimately, a leader is someone who has followers, and others perceive a good leader as effective and organized—a skill that is important in maintaining power and eliciting influence over others (Ewen et al., 2014). The skills required at different management levels will tend to vary. At a lower level, direct supervision, monitoring problems, and managing conflict are essential. In a middle management position, jobs require greater human relation skills to foster cooperative effort in order to motivate and develop subordinate autonomy. At a higher level of management, there is a shift to long-term planning and increased skill necessary to encourage entrepreneurial ability. Executive level managers are expected to promote change on a systematic level and are expected to have more inspirational social qualities (Eagly & Karau, 2002). Individuals in leadership positions must possess a high level of social competency in order to succeed. There are different facets of social intelligence that are highly predictive of leadership success. It was proposed that any type of personality can reach the top but the executives most likely to do so are more likely to prefer extraversion and intuition, and are highly likely to have thinking and judgment traits.

Personality Characteristics

Several books and articles have been dedicated to strategies for the advancement in leadership roles. There is also a large body of research on the personality characteristics most common and effective in the rise in leadership positions (Cole, 1999;

Waniganayake, 2002). The implication behind these results is that leadership skills can be learned and refined and that leaders may have various traits; however, those who rise to the top tend to share certain characteristics. There seem to be differences between leaders and non-leaders on a number of personality attributes (Antonakis, 2004).

Some personality characteristics valued in a leader tend towards assertion, control, and confidence in propensity. A good leader may be aggressive, ambitious, dominant, forceful, independent, self-sufficient, and self-confident (Eagly & Karau, 2002). These characteristics are usually ascribed more strongly to men and may be perceived negatively when employed by women. Women continue to be underrepresented in the highest-level leadership positions despite a similar level of education and related experience as compared to men. Across most industries, at the state level and in the military, women hold a small proportion of leadership roles. Women face more difficulty than men in achieving higher leadership success. The conflict lies in the social pressure to conform to their gender roles which traditional thinkers believe in is contrast to a good leader roles (Eagly & Karau, 2002). A woman who intends to rise in leadership will face more prejudice and challenges if the incongruity between gender roles and leadership is present.

Political Skills

Political skill is suggested to be particularly important as effectively understanding others will allow for more effective influence over them (Ewen et al., 2014). A leader who demonstrates political skill will be more successful in obtaining the favor of their followers. Several agentic qualities are used to describe higher-level successful leadership. Communal characteristics are ascribed more to woman and in terms of leadership include interpersonal sensitivity, and more gentle sympathetic traits, which are less valued in leadership positions in the United States. In other countries, it is more common to hold a more androgynous view of leadership. Agentic qualities include the ability to inspire, make decisions, be courageous, resilient and proactive in addition to using strategic thinking (Eagly & Karau, 2002). These agentic characteristics are more common in middle management positions than they are in lower level management. Due to these perceived gender differences, inequalities in promotion to higher level are prevalent. Although at lower level management, women and men may be nearly equal in salary and title, men are more likely to be promoted.

Due to the perceived gender differences and personality characteristics, men and women are likely to vary in successful methods to achieve higher-ranking leadership positions. Some research suggests that the nature of the industry in question will also determine whether it will be more difficult for a woman to be promoted to a higher level (Eagly & Karau, 2002). Industries that are predominately male or that require more stereotypical male characteristics are less likely to promote women to higher leadership due to the aforementioned conflict in regard to non-conforming gender norms. Women, perhaps due to internalized gender roles, are more likely to employ a democratic leadership style with their subordinates. This leadership strategy appears less powerful and confident and is less likely to be promoted.

The general challenges of career climbing are overtly difficult which makes it increasingly important for both men and women who are looking to move up in their career to research strategies thoroughly. In order to avoid stagnation, a person in a leadership position who is seeking advancement must continue to be active and have a strong sense of ambition if they desire progress. Leaders who wish to get ahead will actively seek out responsibility, power, status, recognition, and individual success.

Setting Yourself Apart

Similar to applying to a new job or starting a career, there are a few key steps that could be beneficial in setting yourself apart from others and thus increasing your visibility and potential as a leader. It will undoubtedly take additional effort and time but simply doing the basics requirements of your position will not be sufficient in getting ahead. A true passion and commitment to your job is exemplary and may even be evident to others but in order to expand other's perception of you as a higher-level leader you must not be afraid to be bold and be vocal. Exhibiting agentic traits like confidence and extraversion will set a tone for others to equate you with well-researched leadership qualities.

Regular attendance of team meetings and involvement in the discussion is a way of showing interest and motivation. As previously stated, it will take more effort than simple doing the basic requirements of your job in order to grow as a leader. Being present and showing up to meetings is important but being a silent observer will not be productive. Voicing well-thought opinions or doing additional research on topics as well as taking certain risks in meetings will make you more memorable.

Another step for growth would be networking with the appropriate circle of individuals that could also help facilitate visibility. Speaking to someone in a higher position and verbalizing interest may allow for opportunities to be presented to you when they become available. A higher level of communication about your own personal goals and how they align with the organization that you work for will validate you as a trusted and valuable member of the team. It may not happen overnight but continued involvement often pays off as long as the quality of work and effort is consistently high. The act of simply stating interest and asking for what you want is grossly underestimated. If you wish to become a leader, you must not be afraid of putting yourself out there.

In summary, certain leadership attributes and personality characteristics are helpful in advancement to higher leadership positions. Social intelligence and confidence are strong indicators of leadership potential. In order to continue in ascend of the leadership ladder, continuing effort and ambition is essential. Actively seeking relationships with peers and mentors will be a necessary way of learning more and establishing yourself in your field. With the respect and support of your peers and with the guidance of those with more experience, you will surely be on the path to increased success. It will not be enough to simply do the basics of your job but you must instead excel and show passion and commitment to the advancement and success of your organization. Proactively asking about open leadership position as well as preparing and applying to those positions will ensure more visibility and respect by those around you. Speaking up at meetings and taking chances by putting yourself and your ideas on display will surely represent your dedication and abilities to those currently in charge.

References

Bardou, K. J., Byrne, H. M., Pasternak, V. S., Perez, N. C., & Rainey, A. L. (2003). Self-efficacy and student leaders: The effects of gender, previous leadership experience, and institutional environment. *Journal of the Indiana University Student Personnel Association, 45*(36), 33–48.

Cole, M. (1999). Become the leader followers want to follow. *Supervision, 60*(12), 9.

Denmark, F. L. (1977). Styles of leadership. *Psychology of Women Quarterly, 2*(2), 99–113. https://doi.org/10.1111/j.1471-6402.1977.tb00493.x.

Denmark, F. L. (1993). Women, leadership, and empowerment. *Psychology of Women Quarterly, 17*(3), 343–356. https://doi.org/10.1111/j.1471-6402.1993.tb00491.x.

Eagly, A. H., & Carli, L. L. (2003). The female leadership advantage: An evaluation of the evidence. *The Leadership Quarterly, 14*(6), 807–834. https://doi.org/10.1016/j.leaqua.2003.09.004.

Eagly, A. H., & Karau, S. J. (2002). Role congruity theory of prejudice toward female leaders. *Psychological Review, 109*(3), 573.

Ewen, C., Wihler, A., Frieder, R. E., Blickle, G., Hogan, R., & Ferris, G. R. (2014). Leader advancement motive, political skill, leader behavior, and effectiveness: A moderated mediation extension of socioanalytic theory. *Human Performance, 27*(5), 373–392.

Goleman, D. (1998, Nov. & Dec.). What makes a Leader? *Harvard Business Review*.

Mayer, A. P., Files, J. A., Ko, M. G., & Blair, J. E. (2008). Academic advancement of women in medicine: Do socialized gender differences have a role in mentoring? *Mayo Clinic Proceedings, 83*(2), 204–207.

Posner, B. Z. (2004). A leadership development instrument for students: Updated. *Journal of College Student Development, 45*(4), 443–456. https://doi.org/10.1353/csd.2004.0051.

Rowe, W. G. (2007). *Cases in leadership*. Los Angeles, CA: Sage.

Schoenberg, J., Salmond, K., & Fleshman, P. (2008). *Change it up!: What girls say about redefining leadership*. New York, NY: Girl Scouts of America.

Waniganayake, M. (2002). Growth of leadership: With training, can anyone become a leader? In *Leadership in early childhood education* (pp. 115–125). Oulu, Finland: University of Oulu.

Zaccaro, S. J., Kemp, C., & Bader, P. (2004). Leader traits and attributes. In J. Antonakis, A. T. Cianciolo, & R. J. Sternberg (Eds.), *The nature of leadership* (pp. 101–124). Thousand Oaks, CA: Sage.

The Important Role of Women in Social Entrepreneurship

Alan Belasen and Joseph Angiello

> *Ignore the glass ceiling and do your work. If you're focusing on the glass ceiling, focusing on what you don't have, focusing on the limitations, then you will be limited. My way was to work, make my short... make my documentary... make my small films... use my own money... raise money myself... and stay shooting and focused on each project.*
>
> Ava Duvernay

Introduction

We need entrepreneurs, broadly conceived, for virtually all of our material, biological, and social needs including food, shelter, entertainment, and the services that we enjoy. And, because entrepreneurs compete with each other in the provision of goods and services and in the facilitation of business transactions, we owe increases in our quality of work life and standards of living, in large part, to these entrepreneurs.

The term "entrepreneurship" in the broad sense of business ownership is derived from a much narrower conception introduced by economists Jean-Baptiste Say in the nineteenth century in which the entrepreneur created value by moving resources to higher planes of production and Joseph Schumpeter who, a century later, identified the entrepreneur as the driving force behind the growth of an economy (Martin, 2007).

Schumpeter distinguished between "adaptive responses," behaviors that fall within the range of accepted practice, and "creative responses," behaviors that fall outside the range of existing practice. According to Schumpeter's theory, creative

A. Belasen (✉) · J. Angiello
MBA Program, SUNY Empire State College, Saratoga Springs, NY, USA
e-mail: abelasen@esc.edu

F. L. Denmark, M. A. Paludi (eds.), *Women and Leadership*,
https://doi.org/10.1007/978-3-319-72182-8_4

responses in business are coterminous with the idea of entrepreneurship and they have several characteristics that distinguish them from adaptive behaviors:

1. Creative responses can't be understood ex-ante, that is, knowing what to do, given a set of existing facts, is not a matter of simple inference;
2. Creative responses shape the "whole course of subsequent events and their long-run outcome"; and
3. Creative responses are related to the abilities of people in society, the abilities of people in relevant industries, and the decisions and actions that they take (Schumpeter, 1947).

Schumpeter points to several distinctions between the capitalist and the entrepreneur and the inventor and the entrepreneur. Although capitalists provide the funds necessary for business and inventors provide ideas that ultimately are converted into products and services, the entrepreneur is the innovator who gets things done. For example, while Henry Ford did not invent the automobile, he systematized its production, making it more reliable and more affordable for average people by dramatically changing the assembly line which he did not invent. Other theorists, like Peter Drucker, writing in the twentieth century, define entrepreneurs as those who create value by recognizing and responding to change rather than the "heroic" change agents that Schumpeter describes (Martin, 2007). It is within this context that we address the empowerment of women in initiating and mobilizing support for social entrepreneurship as a venue for solving problems affecting them and the community. Women entrepreneurs face a variety of issues which can limit their success.

Challenges and Constraints

Until about 20 years ago, entrepreneurship and business leadership were almost exclusively male-dominated activities. The article by Williams (2012) "*Why Women May Be Better Leaders than Men*" brings to light many examples of how women are making significant strides as champions of change and as intrapreneurs in their organizations but still suffer from stereotypical biases, negative evaluations, and lack of recognition—the invisible barriers that separate women and minorities from top leadership positions. The lack of promotion opportunities, limited flexibility on the part of employers, and lack of upward mobility leave many women with untapped potential in their organizations to contemplate career possibilities outside the organization. Belasen (2012) reported a higher turnover rate of women with at least 10 years of executive experience than males at the same level. Between the stress of balancing work and home and other workplace barriers, one can understand why many women feel frustrated when bias-based objections become a reality or when peripheral considerations become the center for vicious office politics and power struggle preventing women from reaching the top.

Women face a catch-22 when they enter professional careers. High-achieving women who attempt to combine work responsibilities with family are either condemned for compromising their familial obligations, or for hindering their full professional potential by spending time and effort around their personal life. Lisa Belkin (2003) of the *New York Times* pointed out an alarming trend—large numbers of highly qualified women dropping out of mainstream careers. Labeling these women the "opt-out revolution," Belkin traces the reasons and provides evidence that women steer onto the off-ramp at some point on their career pathway.

Empirical evidence confirms that women in leadership positions help improve organizational performance and stakeholder satisfaction, yet the support systems such as flexible work schedules, maternity leaves, and re-entry on the fast track for promotion are lacking. High-achieving women are not meeting their career goals not because they decide to opt out of the workforce due to their caregiving responsibilities but rather due to the inflexibility of workplaces' policies and practices. Until companies mainstream flexible arrangements, the talents and skills of high-potential women will continue to be directed towards external goals including social entrepreneurship.

A study by John Becker-Blease from Oregon State University that was conducted in 2010 found that about 7.2% of high-achieving women left their jobs, compared to 3.8% of men. Both the voluntary rates (4.3% versus 2.8% for men) and the involuntary rates (2.9% versus 0.9%) were higher for women executives. Women are more likely to leave their jobs due to domestic obligations or because of higher social consciousness than men, which could explain the higher-than-men voluntary departure rate (Klampe, 2010). Women tend to stay away from management positions due to lack of workplace flexibility (15%) and placing a bigger priority on family (26%), but also because of institutional barriers and lack of mobility (42%), less willingness to take risks (10%), and lack of mentoring and social support, estimated at 7% (Inam, 2013). The constraints on women from entering executive suites and corporate boardrooms, paradoxically, has also created opportunities for women to apply their innovativeness and creativity skills elsewhere, primarily the formation of startups, the subject of subsequent sections.

The Second Glass Ceiling

Bosse and Taylor (2012) proposed that the second glass ceiling appears like an entrepreneurship corollary to the first glass ceiling (the invisible barrier that separates women and minorities from top leadership position) except that it centers on the capital markets that serve small firms. They pointed out that women entrepreneurs face tighter credit availability from financial institutions to start new firms or to fuel the growth of existing small firms. For example, the *Center for Women's Business Research's Women Confidence Index* reported in 2010 that women business owners continue to cite problems of getting loans. Bosse and Taylor (2012) agreed that more women business owners are seeking credit, but fewer report that they are getting all of the credit they want (9.5% in 2009 versus 6.3% in 2010) and more report that they are getting none of the credit they want (20% in 2009 versus

25% in 2010). Even for firms with higher annual revenues (greater than $500,000) only 10.3% in 2010 received all the credit they wanted, while 65.5% stated that they were able to obtain at least some, most, or all credit sought. In contrast, only a third (33.3%) of those with smaller annual revenues (less than $500,000) were able to obtain at least some, most, or all credit sought.

The use of ***gender as a grouping criterion*** is widely observed in sociological research. People feel most comfortable working with others who manifest similar characteristics, personal traits, or behaviors. Thus, as long as there are many more males than females at banks and investment firms in positions to allocate financial capital, it follows that males who seek capital may receive a disproportionate share, ceteris paribus. Even as women-owned businesses continue to grow at rates exceeding the national average in the USA, these firms have not been moving along the growth continuum (American Express, 2011). Men-owned businesses, on average, are larger than women-owned businesses—about twice as many than women-owned businesses have ten or more employees and three times as many have reached the $1 million revenue mark (American Express, 2011).

Traits and Skills

Bellucci, Borisov, and Zazzaro (2010) found that women business managers tend to perceive critical decision events as riskier and are more risk-averse than men, particularly in the area of financial investments. This was corroborated by Hadary (2010) who suggested that the stereotype that women are perceived as incapable of leading substantial, growing businesses is pervasive among business and government leaders. She also pointed to women's own perceptions of incompetence as a key reason why others do not believe their firms will grow. Bosse and Taylor (2012) cite strong evidence from a multi-country database of 14,000 firms that shows that women-managed firms are 5% less likely to get a bank loan approved compared to men and when they do get a bank loan, on average, they pay half a percentage point more in interest (Muravyev, Talavera, & Schafer, 2009). Furthermore, analysis of a longitudinal survey of almost 5000 entrepreneurial firms shows that not only do women get significantly less external debt and equity than men at firm startup; they also get significantly less capital in the subsequent 2 years (Coleman & Robb, 2009).

As in politics, entrepreneurship is associated with male characteristics such as assertiveness and self-promotion, tactics used to control impressions and exercise influence. Thus, the possession of political skills or lack thereof can be predictive of women's success as entrepreneurs. For this reason, Phipps and Prieto (2015) found that males have greater propensity than females to be entrepreneurs. Also, the limited presence of women entrepreneurs means that female mentors are not available to support and encourage the self-efficacy of would-be female entrepreneurs. Since creativity is positively correlated with entrepreneurial intentions (Hamidi, Wennberg & Berglund, 2008; Olawale, 2010; Phipps, 2012), this, too, could be a determinant of entrepreneurial self-efficacy.

Geibel, Askari, and Heinzel (2014) used The Global Entrepreneurship Monitor (2009 GEM Report) to measure the "fear of failure rate" in 26 countries. This rate is defined as the percentage of the age of "18–64 of population with positive perceived opportunities who indicate that fear of failure would prevent them from setting up a business." In 2012, 27% of the individuals with entrepreneurial aspirations in the USA recognized opportunities but did not follow through on their plans, even if the expected utility was projected to be higher than the next best alternative. Factors contributing to this fear included the availability of startup capital (liquidity constraints), economic growth (level of industrialization, employment), entrepreneurship education (building skills and knowledge of entrepreneurship), reputation (image), and startup activity (level of involvement). One of the findings was that even if the economy of a country is well developed, a recession might raise the fear of failure due to the negative development and prevent people from starting a business. Furthermore, a low startup activity increases the fear of failure rate. Possibly, individuals who are currently not involved in a startup have less confidence concerning the potential of their ideas if they don't observe other people being successful or trying to be successful. Observing a higher degree of entrepreneurial activity could raise their trust in the market conditions required for successfully setting up their own business.

The Reality

These obstacles to female entrepreneurship, notwithstanding, did not discourage women from pursuing social innovation. If anything else, it showed that women-owned business is a force to be reckoned with. While an average of 506 new women-owned firms were started each day since 2007, the daily average was 602 per day from 2011 to 2012, 744 per day from 2012 to 2013, and fully 1288 per day in 2014—showing that the number of new women-owned firms launched each day has doubled over just a few years. From 2007 to 2014, the number of women-owned firms increased by 17% compared to an overall increase in new firms of 13%—a ratio of 1.3:1. As mentioned earlier, over the entire 1997–2014 period, the number of women-owned firms has increased at a rate 1½ times the national average (Womenable, 2014). About 50% of all new establishments survive 5 years or more and about one-third of the new startups survive 10 years or more.

In 2014, there were 9.1 million women-owned firms, employing 7.9 million workers and generating $1.4 trillion in revenues (Womenable, 2014). The "death" rates were lower for female-owned establishments than male-owned establishments for enterprises of 50 or more employees (United States Department of Commerce Economics and Statistics Administration, 2010). Although the total number of new establishments has not been growing as it did before the 2007 economic downturn and the number has actually been much lower than it was during the 2001 recession, the number of women-owned firms has increased, as noted above, more than the overall "birth" rate of new business. Between the higher "birth" rate and the lower "death" rate, the percent of women-owned businesses has been growing.

The growth of female-owned businesses suggests that the prospects for women in business are generally getting better. The *Small Business Administration's Office of Advocacy* (2014) defines a small business as an independent business having fewer than 500 employees. In 2011, there were 28.2 million small businesses representing 99.7% of the US firms, 63% of net new private-sector jobs, 48.5% of private-sector employment, 42% of private-sector payroll, 46% of private-sector output, 37% of high-tech employment, 98% of firms exporting goods, and 33% of exporting value. How much of this activity is conducted by women-owned firms? As of 2014, there were nearly 9.1 million women-owned businesses in the United States, accounting for 37.8% of all small business generating over $1.4 trillion in revenues and employing nearly 7.9 million people.

While women-owned firms remain smaller than male-owned firms in terms of average employment and revenues, they are not only showing higher percent growth in numbers but also higher absolute growth in terms of job creation adding an estimated 274,000 jobs since 2007. For comparison, employment in men-owned and equally owned firms has declined over the past 7 years. Between 1997 and 2014, when the number of businesses in the United States increased by 47%, the number of women-owned firms increased by 68%—a rate 145% greater than the national average. Indeed, the growth in the number (up 68%), employment (up 11%), and revenues (up 72%) of women-owned firms from 1997 to 2014 exceeded the growth rates of all but the largest publicly traded firms (Womenable, 2014). More than 75% of female-owned businesses operate in service and retail industries in which women's attributes and inner capabilities appear advantageous.

Resources to Support Female Entrepreneurship

Probably, the best evidence that female entrepreneurship is here to stay is the burgeoning growth of resources devoted to its support. Here are some examples. The Goldman Sach's 10,000 Women Initiative was created with the goal of educating women entrepreneurs in emerging economies. The program helps women to reach their entrepreneurial goals and, in turn, stimulate the overall economy in the communities that these men serve. By the close of 2013, the initiative had enrolled its 10,000th woman (Babson College, 2014). Similarly, the *Coca-Cola 5by20* campaign was launched in 2010 to help women reach their entrepreneurial goals and create sustainable economic climates in their communities by providing them access to business skills, financial services, assets, and support networks. The name *5by20* comes from Coca-Cola's goal of positively affecting five million women by 2020. The campaign currently has programs in 12 countries (Coca Cola, 2013). Recently, Dell launched the "Pay it Forward" initiative to use the power of women's networks to expand opportunities for women entrepreneurs (Dell, Inc., 2013). The campaign works on the premise that if women reciprocate in helping other women achieve their business goals, they can create a global community of women supporting women and these efforts will create a ripple effect. Through this process, Dell has set a goal to track support for 1 million women entrepreneurs by the end of 2015. According to Ingrid Vanderveldt, a well-respected American businesswoman, media personality and investor: "empowering women worldwide and investing in their futures can help drive growth in the global economy and promote economic vitality and security" (2014).

Another female education and funding foundation is Tory Burch. The high-end fashion brand is most popularly known for its classic ballet flat embossed with the gold Tory Burch crest. According to *Forbes* magazine, Tory Burch is worth about $1 billion (Kanani, 2014). Because early on Burch endured the challenges of balancing life-work goals along with the systemic barrier of securing funding, she decided to launch the "Tory Burch Foundation" in 2009, in order to support female entrepreneurs in overcoming their own obstacles. The foundation offers access to capital for loans, specifically through Bank of America through community lenders (Kanani, 2014). It also offers business education, mentoring and networking opportunities. Funding is selective. In order to be eligible, entrepreneurs must have $500,000 in annual revenues.

While there are many barriers hindering women from reaching their entrepreneurial goals, there are also many programs out there with the sole intent of funding women's business ideas. Those mentioned here are only a few of them.

The Intellectual Boundaries of Social Entrepreneurship

Whereas private enterprise and, by extension, entrepreneurship are typically focused on profits and not social problems, social entrepreneurship is more narrowly focused on social problems; it addresses an undesirable equilibrium that relegates people to lives of deprivation and uncertainty about their prospects for the future. "Unlike the entrepreneurial value proposition that assumes a market that can pay for the innovation, and may even provide substantial upside for investors, the social entrepreneur's value proposition targets an under-served, neglected, or highly disadvantaged population that lacks the financial means or political clout to achieve the trans-formative benefit on its own". The ascendency of "pro-poor" policy as a guiding principle in economic development is one outward manifestation of the quest for this new equilibrium. According to Martin (2007, p. 32) "…the entrepreneur is attracted to this suboptimal equilibrium, seeing embedded in it an opportunity to provide a new solution, product, service, or process. The reason that the entrepreneur sees this condition as an opportunity to create something new, while so many others see it as an inconvenience to be tolerated, stems from the unique set of personal characteristics he or she brings to the situation—inspiration, creativity, direct action, courage, and fortitude. These characteristics are fundamental to the process of innovation."

As suggested earlier, there are a number of conceptions of "social entrepreneurship." A useful taxonomy is offered by Dees and Anderson (2006) who suggest that the definitions fall into two categories: the social enterprise school and the social innovation school.

In the view of those in the social enterprise school, a social entrepreneur runs a socially oriented business or takes a market-based approach to a societal problem. In the view of those in the social innovation school, a social entrepreneur is a change champion who seeks large-scale, sustainable changes, as discussed in connection with Schumpeter above, to improve society. In the words of Martin (2007, pp. 34–35), "…the social entrepreneur aims for value in the form of large-scale, transformational benefit that accrues either to a significant segment of society or to society at large." Bornstein (2007) distinguished social entrepreneurs as a transformational force: Relentless individuals with practical vision, stamina, and persistence to achieve their goals and spread their ideas. Indeed, women social entrepreneurs manifest these views.

Convergent definitions suggest that social entrepreneurs are found in all walks of life, in all societal sectors; their goal is to address a serious social problem and that they possess traits that set them apart from other well-meaning people who want to make a difference in the world: Social entrepreneurs are *not* simply businesspeople solving social ills, but people with innovative thinking spreading new approaches—through nonprofits and businesses, or within government—to address emergent and new problems successfully (Bornstein, 2012).

Commonly conceived, social entrepreneurship encompasses a vision for society that has the following elements:

- Social entrepreneurship is an innovative initiative that addresses societal problems that, heretofore, have been inadequately addressed.
- The goal of social entrepreneurship is to create a better society.
- While profit is not the focus of social entrepreneurship, it is not inconsistent with making a profit; in fact, since there is a growing recognition that societal problems require partnerships involving business, government, and the nonprofit sector, social entrepreneurship could well involve profit-making.
- Social entrepreneurship requires innovative, even revolutionary, business approaches that achieve sufficient scope and scale to be effective and sustainable.

So defined, the types of individuals who envision improving society may come from different backgrounds, training, and orientations; they may have different world views and motives for what they do; they may use different methods and structures to accomplish their objectives. These efforts may be undertaken by businesses, nonprofit organizations, or the government, though, increasingly, successful social entrepreneurship will probably require collaboration of more than one, possibly, all of these sectors. Examples of business organizations that meet this definition would include Ben and Jerry's Ice Cream, Newman's Own products, and Grameen Bank. Examples of individuals who were the force behind profound societal change include Dorothea Dix who raised consciousness about and developed practices for treating the mentally ill; A. Philip Randolph who led black porters and maids in forming a union and was a key figure in the civil rights movement; Gifford Pinchot who is considered by many to be the "father" of the conservation movement in the United States and was one of the first to introduce the idea of renewable resources and sustainability; Susan B. Anthony who fought for women's rights; and Florence Nightingale who established modern nursing and the first school to train nurses.

Based on this definition, social entrepreneurship should not to be confused with the work of charitable organizations or mutual benefit associations which are more aptly termed "social enterprises" (Dees and Anderson 2006) than "social innovators" although they are still important institutions and there could well be overlap in the work of and alliances between charities and social innovators.

As Wei-Skillern, Austin, Leonard, and Stevenson (2007, p. 4) so aptly summed up these ideas, social entrepreneurship is an "...innovative, social value-creating activity that can occur within or across the nonprofit, business or government sector."

Why Is Social Entrepreneurship Necessary?

American capitalism has produced an enormous amount of wealth, bestowing a high standard of living and life expectancy creating a huge middle class out of people who, in centuries past, would have lived lives of deprivation with very little separating them from starvation and death at a young age. Between World War II and 1970, the percentage of income increase of Americans across the income spectrum grew fairly evenly and dramatically, doubling over that period. However, the average American household has essentially the same income as in 1970 though it takes two wage earners to secure the same income, adjusted for inflation, and the distribution of income is very uneven. In 2013, the top 3% received 31% of total income and 54% of total wealth (Stone, 2015).

In addition, even as the USA enters its eighth year of economic growth since the Great Recession in 2007–2008, many people remain either unemployed or underemployed and some have become so discouraged that they have either abandoned their search for employment or have settled for part-time work. Capitalism is blind to their needs. And the fact that the skills of American workers have been slipping in comparison to people in many other industrial countries does not suggest that things will improve appreciably for average Americans in the near future. The convergence of these and other events has led to the greatest amount of income and wealth inequality that the United States has ever seen, with fewer and fewer people receiving more and more income and wealth. What a dichotomy! The American economy is doing just fine while average people and their children, who make up a disproportionate number of the American poor, struggle.

In addition, the "nonexcludability" feature of public goods obviates the profit incentive and the solution to problems that might, otherwise, be eliminated. This has left a significant portion of the country's population poor, without adequate medical care, without adequate education and, in some cases, few prospects for improvement. Indeed, capitalism itself creates many problems in the form of spillovers such as pollution, illness, and stress.

Problems have always existed but, besides those mentioned above, several pernicious, secular trends are increasing the need for new approaches within nonprofit, government, and business organizations but, also, approaches that necessarily involve the intimate cooperation of the three sectors:

- The degradation of our natural environmental
- The increasing costs of education and the strain this imposes on average people
- The gulf between those who have information technology and those who don't
- The lagging school performance of the poor as well Blacks and Hispanics
- The burgeoning cost of health care and the concomitant increase in health problems
- Deteriorating prospects for the escape from intergenerational poverty

These problems, increasingly, require bold and inventive solutions characterized by Schumpeterian entrepreneurship but, at the same time, more explicitly anchored in the creation of public value. They will not yield to simple good intentions. If they did, they would no longer exist given the spectacular increase in the nonprofit and governmental sectors in the last few decades.

While the government and nonprofit organizations are bastions against problems that the free market has not solved and has even contributed to, these sectors are beset with their own problems. Governmental agencies at all levels are constrained by demands for limited government and resistance to transfer payments and are less able, in real dollar terms, to support nonprofit organizations; worse, they have increasingly passed unfunded mandates to the nonprofit sector. As for their part, while nonprofit and nongovernmental organizations provide badly needed social services, they must appeal largely to third parties who do not directly benefit from their activity for a large share of their funding and they are often hampered by inadequate business-related skills such as the ability to develop scalable offerings.

According to the *National Center for Charitable Statistics*, there are over 1.5 million 501(c) organizations which account for approximately 10% of all American wages and salaries. Although the number of these nonprofit organizations has continued to grow, the growth has created more competition among them. Accordingly, there is great flux among these organizations, with approximately 16% disappearing over a 5-year period, many probably going out of existence. Though, over time, their revenues have kept pace with inflation, they are in a constant quest for new funds (McKeever, 2016). The results of one study of the problems facing the nonprofit sector are instructive:

- Many development director positions remain vacant for many months; the median vacancy length is 6 months with 46% of all nonprofits reporting even longer vacancy lengths;
- Many nonprofit development officers consider their jobs a setup because of the considerable constraints they face including untrained and unsupportive boards;
- Half of all development officers anticpiate leaving their jobs within 2 years; one quarter anticipate leaving the field within 2 years;

- One quarter of the executives of nonprofits are not satisfied with the skills of their development officers. Many say the talent does not exist in the labor pool. These numbers are higher for smaller organizations;
- Smaller organizations are unable to compete with larger, with nonprofits with budgets up to $1 million paying development officers approximately $49,000 and the largest nonprofits paying over $100,000 (Bell, 2013).

America needs new approaches to its social problems, approaches that are built upon the same type of innovativeness and vision that has driven American business but that have societal problems as their focus and rely on cooperation across all three societal sectors—business, the government, and the nonprofit community. Social entrepreneurship may be a step in that direction.

The Growth of Social Entrepreneurship

Fortunately, there is evidence that social entrepreneurship is growing dramatically. It is impossible to quantify this precisely, largely because social entrepreneurship manifests itself across all sectors and many job titles and because we are nowhere near universal agreement on the precise definition of social entrepreneurship. Nevertheless, there are a number of tangible, quantifiable indications that the interest in social goals is growing and, with it, the need for particular business competencies, buttressed by an understanding of societal issues, social justice, and organizational models that involve partnerships between and among business, nonprofits, and the government. These indicators include the following:

- The number of academic programs, courses, and institutes relating to social sector management or that contain social benefit content is burgeoning. Between 1993 and 2011, the Harvard Business School alone produced approximately 600 cases and books on social entrepreneurship and approximately 600 students enrolled in social enterprise courses and initiatives; each year more than 500 practitioners participate in the HBS's Social Enterprise Executive Education Institute; 1/3 of HBS alumni serve on nonprofit boards; HSB's Social Enterprise Club, with 400 members, is one of the school's largest student clubs; HBS alumni clubs provide $10M annually in pro bono consulting work for social initiatives (Milway & Goulay, 2013).
- The top colleges in the country have doubled their courses relating to managing in the social sector since 2003; 95% of Yale School of Management courses contain social content; the mission of Yale's School of Management is focused on "turning out not only business leaders but leaders for society" (Milway & Goulay, 2013).
- Whereas in the mid-nineties, in mid-level colleges in the USA and Canada, there was only one full program focused on social entrepreneurship, in 2005 there were hundreds of courses and 30 colleges offered full-fledged programs in social entrepreneurship (Hahn, 2005). No doubt, today the number is much higher.

- The business sector's interest in corporate social responsibility has increased exponentially as businesses focus on the triple bottom line and increasingly include social goals in their strategic planning, support their employees in meeting the needs of their communities and establish foundations that give money to for-profit and nonprofit organizations that take on issues with a social purpose. Businesses recognize that this is not only the right thing to do but that it also drives innovation and promotes learning and adds to their bottom line. According to a McKinsey survey, "Valuing Corporate Social Responsibility," environmental, social, and governance programs have soared in recent years, as executives, investors, and regulators have grown increasingly aware that such programs can mitigate corporate crises and build reputations… "Solid majorities of all respondents expect environmental, social, and governance programs to create more value in the next five years" (McKinsey and Company, 2009).
- Not surprisingly, American consumers indirectly support the development of social entrepreneurship by demanding goods provided by socially responsive companies, though they may have to pay a premium for these goods. According to a 2013 Nielsen survey, 50% of consumers compared to 45% in 2011 were willing to pay more for products from companies that are trying to give back to society. Though this is a sentiment most associated with people under 30, it is growing among all age groups, among men as well as women, and across the 58 countries surveyed (Nielsen, 2013).

Writing in 2007, Charles Leadbeater, a pioneer in the field of social entrepreneurship education offered the following observations which outline nicely the progress it made in the previous decade, the need for it, and the direction the field needed to take:

Ten years ago, social entrepreneurs "were a ragtag group of misfits and mavericks, heroic figures, seemingly single-handedly bringing jobs, healthcare and education to deprived communities" with only one school for social entrepreneurs. Now, the "movement" is supported by 30 universities around the world with full-fledged programs and, whereas social entrepreneurship is usually a team effort, it is "fed by an eclectic mix of church groups, venture capitalists, philanthropists, former political activists, community businesses, and the rise of corporate social responsibility."

Third sector social enterprise organizations alone employ around 40 million people worldwide and have 200 million volunteers.

The social entrepreneurship "movement" has increasingly helped itself. Building on the efforts of the pioneer organization, Ashoka, which has recognized and given material support to thousands of social entrepreneurs, many similarly committed organizations have emerged, including Skoll and Schwab and the Community Action Network.

The biggest challenge facing the social sector is figuring out how to scale up its impact, acquire capital, and increase its management skills.

The potential for the growth of social collaboration is enormous, as the internet has opened up new avenues for entrepreneurs in what could become a mass activity (Leadbeater, 2007).

Finally, the federal government and several states have formalized their recognition of social entrepreneurship and the need for it. At the federal level, the Office of Innovation and Entrepreneurship has been established within the *United States Department of Commerce*, "to foster a more innovative US economy focused on turning new ideas and inventions into products and technologies that spur job growth and competitiveness while promoting economic development" (U.S. Economic Development Agency, 2016).

At the state level, several states allow the creation of a brand new form of business organization, the benefit organization. The benefit organization is allowed to make a profit, unlike 501 (c) (3) organizations, as they pursue social missions. The organization must appoint a benefit officer who must report yearly that the organization has, indeed, carried out its mission.

Conclusion: The Role of Women in Entrepreneurship

As discussed earlier, private enterprise has been the almost exclusive province of men. Although women have made steady progress in closing the pay gap, there is still a significant pay gap between men and women; and although women are better represented in management positions than they have been, women are noticeable by their absence from executive suites and boardrooms. However, women have played a much more significant role in distinguishing themselves as social entrepreneurs and are almost as likely as men to be social entrepreneurs. We are not surprised by this and we argue that women, because of their orientation, sensibilities, and skill sets, are uniquely prepared to provide leadership in the quest for equality, fairness, and sustainability that have remained so vexingly out of reach even for the United States and most advanced economies.

Whereas the literature on market-based activity has focused on self-utility maximization and profit seeking behavior, social enterprises seek to create social value and are largely driven by the "other-oriented" motivation of compassion (Miller, Grimes, McMullen, & Vogus, 2012). Compassion is the vital "other-oriented" motivator that "fosters integrative solutions to seemingly intractable social problems…and encourages the commitment needed to undertake demanding and difficult responses." And… "compassion, when combined with the perceived legitimacy of social entrepreneurship, increases the likelihood of launching a social enterprise" (Miller et al., 2012, p. 618).

In this conjuncture, it is interesting to note that, whereas men dominate mainstream (market-based) entrepreneurship and are twice as likely to set up a conventional business organization, women set up social entrepreneurial enterprises almost as often as men (Harding, 2004). This resonates well with studies of the role of gender in career selection. Women disproportionately select certain careers and have distinctly different long-term goals or visions for their future (Evans & Diekman, 2009). "…women, more than men, tend to endorse the values of benevolence and universalism, whereas men more than women, tend to endorse the values of power and achievement, self-direction and stimulation" (Evans & Diekman, p. 237). While the "soft" skills and values (e.g., creativity, energy, and compassion) are difficult to develop, they are also congruent with women's characteristics and the overarching purpose of social entrepreneurship as evident in the success stories and outcomes of women's initiatives described earlier in the chapter. Other aspects of entrepreneurial skills (or hard skills such as business planning and capital options, the primary domain of men's skills) can be learned and nourished by women through training and education (Belasen & Frank, 2012). Fittingly, these roles and skills, dispositional or learned, are predictive of women's abilities to initiate and champion social entrepreneurship ventures.

References

American Express. (2011). *The American Express OPEN state of women-owned business report: A summary of important trends, 1997-2011*. New York City, NY: American Express.

Babson College. (2014). *Investing in the power of women—A report on the 10,000 women program*. Babson Park, MA: Babson College.

Belasen, A. (2012). *Developing women leaders in Corporate America: Balancing competing demands, transcending traditional boundaries*. Santa Barbara, CA: Praeger.

Belasen, A., & Frank, N. (2012). Using the competing values framework to evaluate the interactive effects of gender and personality traits on leadership. *International Journal of Leadership Studies, 7*(2), 192–215.

Belkin, L. (2003, October 26). *The opt-out revolution*. Retrieved from New York Times Magazine: http://www.nytimes.com/2003/10/26/magazine/26WOMEN.html?pagewanted=all.

Bell, J. (2013, April 6). *Underdeveloped: A national study of challenges facing nonprofit fundraising*. San Francisco, CA: CompassPoint Nonprofit Services and the Evelyn and Walter Haas, Jr. Fund. Retrieved from National Council of Nonprofits: http://www.giarts.org/sites/default/files/Underdeveloped-National-Study-of-Challenges-Facing-Nonprofit-Fundraising.pdf.

Bellucci, A. B., Borisov, A., & Zazzaro, A. (2010). Does gender matter in bank-firm relationships? Evidence from small business lending. *Journal of Banking and Finance, 34*, 2968–2984.

Bornstein, D. (2007). *How to change the world: Social entrepreneurs and the power of new ideas*. New York, NY: Oxford University Press.

Bornstein, D. (2012, November 13). The rise of the social entrepreneur. *The New York Times Opinionator*, p. np.

Bosse, D., & Taylor, P. L., III. (2012, June). The second glass ceiling impedes women entrepreneurs. *The Journal of Applied Management and Entrepreneurship, 17*(1), 51–68.

Center for Women's Business Research. (2010, June 10). *Center for Women's Business Research*. Retrieved from Key4Women Confidence Index. https://www.key.com/pdf/women-confidence-index-summer10.pdf.

Coca Cola. (2013, March 11). *Coca Cola*. Retrieved from The Coca-Cola Company and IFC Announce Initiative to Support Women Entrepreneurs Across Emerging Markets: http://www.coca-colacompany.com/press-center/press-releases/the-coca-cola-company-and-ifc-announce-initiative-to-support-women-entrepreneurs-across-emerging-markets/.

Coleman, S., & Robb, A. (2009). A comparison of new firm financing by gender: Evidence from the Kaufman Firm Survey Data. *Small Business Economics, 33*, 397–411.

Dees, J., & Anderson, B. (2006). Framing a theory of social entrepreneurship: Building on two schools of practice and thought. In R. Mosher-Williams (Ed.), Research on social entrepreneurship[: Understanding and contributing to an emerging field. *ARMOVA Occasional Paper Series, 1 (3)*, 39-66.

Dell, Inc. (2013, June 3). *Dell, Inc.* Retrieved from Dell launches Pay It Forward initiative to support one million female entrepreneurs by 2015: http://www.dell.com/learn/us/en/uscorp1/secure/2013-06-03-dell-pay-it-forward.

Evans, C. D., & Diekman, A. B. (2009). On motivated role selection: Gender, beliefs, distant goals and career interest. *Psychology of Women Quarterly, 33*, 235–249.

Geibel, R. A., Askari, H., & Heinzel, J. (2014). Identification of factors that prevent potential entrepreneurs from founding. *Journal on Business Review, 3*(4), 27–33.

Hadary, S. (2010, May 17). What's holding back women entrepreneurs? *The Wall Street Journal*. pp. R1, R3.

Hahn, R. (2005, April nd). Social enterprise goes to school. *Social Enterprise Reporter*. pp. 1–13.

Hamidi, D. Y., Wennberg, K., & Berglund, H. (2008). Creativity in entrepreneurship education. *Journal of Small Business and Enterprise Development, 15*(2), 304–320.

Harding, R. (Winter 2004). Social enterprise: The new economic engine? *Business Strategy Review, 15*(4), 39–43.

Inam, H. (2013, April 15). Retrieved from Transformational Leadership Coaching and Development: http://www.transformleaders.tv/why-arent-there-more-women-ceos/.

Kanani, R. (2014). *Why Tory Burch wants to empower women entrepreneurs*. Retrieved from Forbes Magazine: http://www.forbes.com/sites/rahimkanani/2014/02/20/why-tory-burch-wants-to-empower-women-entrepreneurs/>.

Klampe, M. (2010, October 4). *Women executives twice as likely to leave their jobs as men*. Retrieved from Oregon State University: http://oregonstate.edu/ua/ncs/archives/2010/oct/women-executives-twice-likely-leave-their-jobs-men.

Leadbeater, C. (2007, March 25). *Mainstreaming the Mavericks*. Retrieved from The Guardian: http://www.theguardian.com/society/2007/mar/25/voluntarysector.business.

Martin, R. L. (2007). Social entrepreneurship: The case for definition. *Stanford Social Innovation Review, 5*(2), 28–39.

McKeever, B. T. (2016, April 5). *The nonprofit sector in brief 2015: Public charities, giving and volunteering*. Retrieved from The National Center for Charitable Statistics: http://nccs.urban.org/statistics/quickfacts.cfm.

McKinsey and Company. (2009). *Valuing corporate social responsibility: McKinsey global survey results*. New York, NY: McKinsey and Company.

Miller, T. L., Grimes, M. G., McMullen, J. S., & Vogus, T. J. (2012). Venturing for others with heart and head: How compassion encourages social entrepreneurship. *Academy of Management Review, 37*(4), 616–640.

Milway, K. S., & Goulay, C. D. (2013, March). The rise of social entrepreneurship in B Schools in three charts. Retrieved from The Bridgespan Group: Collaborating to Accelerate Social Impact: http://www.bridgespan.org/Blogs/The-Knowledge-Hopper/March-2013/The-Rise-of-Social-Entrepreneurship-in-B-Schools-i.aspx#.VwecsZeDsnJ.

Muravyev, A. T., Talavera, O., & Schafer, D. (2009). Entrepreneurs' gender and financial constraints: evidence from international data. *Journal of Comparative Economics, 37*(2), 270–286.

Nielsen. (2013). *50% of global consumers surveyed willing to pay more for goods, services from socially responsible companies, up from 2011*. New York City, NY: Nielsen.

Olawale, F. (2010). Graduate entrepreneurial intention in South Africa: Motivations and obstacles. *International Journal of Business, 5*(9), 87–98.

Phipps, S. (2012). Contributors to an enterprising gender: Examining the influence of creativity on entrepreneurial intentions and the moderating role of political skill controlling for gender. *Academy of Entrepreneurship Journal, 18*(1), 77–90.

Phippe, S., & Prieto, L. (2015). Women versus men in entrepreneurship: A comparison of the sexes on creativity, political skill, and entrepreneurial intentions. *Academy of Entrepreneurship Journal, 21*, 32–43.

Schumpeter, J. (1947). Creative response in economic history. *Journal of Economic History, 7*(2), 149–159.

Small Business Administration Office of Advocacy. (2014, March). *Frequently asked questions*. Retrieved from Small Business Administration Office of Advocacy: https://www.sba.gov/sites/default/files/FAQ_March_2014_0.pdf.

Stone, C. T. (2015, October 26). *A guide to statistics on historical trends in income inequality*. Retrieved from Center on Budget and Policy Priorities: http://www.cbpp.org/research/poverty-and-inequality/a-guide-to-statistics-on-historical-trends-in-income-inequality.

Tory Burch Foundation. (n.d.). Retrieved from http://www.toryburchfoundation.org/programs/.

U.S. Economic Development Agency. (2016, May 12). *Office of innovation and entrepreneurship*. Retrieved from U.S. Economic Development Agency: https://www.eda.gov/OIE/.

United States Department of Commerce Economics and Statistics Administration. (2010, October). *Women-owned businesses in the 21st century*. Washington, DC: United States Department of Commerce Economics and Statistics Administration. Retrieved from http://www.esa.doc.gov/sites/default/files/women-owned-businesses.pdf.

Vanderveldt, I. (2014, June 6). *United Nations Foundation*. Retrieved from Resolutions: Female entrepreneurs are key to sustainable global development: http://www.unfoundation.org/blog/female-entrepreneurs.html?referrer=https%3A%2F%2Fwww.google.com%2F.

Wei-Skillern, J. A., Austin, J., Leonard, H., & Stevenson, H. (2007). *Entrepreneurship in the social sector*. New York, NY: Sage.

Williams, R. (2012, December 15). *Why women may be better leaders than men*. Retrieved from Psychology Today: https://www.psychologytoday.com/blog/wired-success/201212/why-women-may-be-better-leaders-men.

Womenable. (2014, March). *2014 report on the state of women-owned businesses report*. Retrieved from Womenable.com: http://www.womenable.com/content/userfiles/2014_State_of_Women-owned_Businesses_public.pdf.

Focus Group Becomes Support Group: Women in Educational Leadership

Jennifer L. Martin, Martina L. Sharp-Grier, and Chloe E. Bortmas

If you are sitting around the table but you say nothing, that's a lost opportunity. Move beyond that and say something about what you have to offer. The reason you're there is because you have something valuable that can be added.

Ursula Burns

Introduction

The myth of meritocracy and denials of inequality still pervade American culture on many levels. The notion that individuals in leadership position are the most deserving of said positions is ubiquitous in our current milieu. However, research indicates that stereotypes, stereotype threat, overt discrimination, and more covert forms of discrimination, such as exposure to daily microaggressions, can render the road to leadership fraught with potholes, pitfalls, and impediments for women, particularly those possessing additional nondominant identities or multiple minority statuses (Gutierrez y Muhs, Flores Niemann, Gonzalez, & Harris, 2012). Yet and still, we are in need of diverse leaders in our educational institutions (Paludi & Coates, 2011), most specifically women.

J. L. Martin (✉) • C. E. Bortmas
Alliance, OH, USA

M. L. Sharp-Grier
North Canton, OH, USA

F. L. Denmark, M. A. Paludi (eds.), *Women and Leadership*,
https://doi.org/10.1007/978-3-319-72182-8_5

Vignette One: The Value of Women's Voices, the Escapades of Jen and Ken

I worked in a high school setting for 17 years; 15 of those years I spent in a small alternative school for students labeled at-risk for school failure. It may or may not be surprising to note, depending on how much one is versed in K-12 education, how many of my co-workers were female. In fact, other than the principal and one other teacher, both male, the rest of my co-workers were female. That is why I found it so interesting when the women around the lunch table would lean in any time the man would say anything. Women even made him lunch and bought him gifts, simply because he was the only man; these were not romantic gestures, but some kind of an antiquated tradition of "kissing the ring," acknowledging the phallus, upholding the patriarchy. My feminist sensibilities were troubled. Sometimes, it was funny. Other times I was incredulous or outraged. And this male teacher was my friend. He would laugh about it, but he did not see at first that it was because of male privilege that he was receiving these gifts, until I pointed it out. At staff meetings, it was not uncommon for me to notice how everything Ken said was lauded. Often, I was ignored. And the majority of the people facing me were female. I understood that women could internalize sexism, so I enlisted Ken into an informal experiment. I explained to him the pattern that I was noticing: men's voices, although in the minority: in this case Ken and the principal, were more valued around the table than were women's. It was not that he did not believe me; he just never noticed it. (He did not have to, as it did not affect him.) Being my friend, and open to my feminist perspective, he agreed to my "experiment." My idea was this: I would broach various ideas during staff meetings. Upon being ignored or dismissed, Ken would broach the exact same idea, worded in a similar manner a few moments later. We repeated this pattern over several weeks and recorded our findings. Although Ken was surprised, I was not. Overwhelmingly, my ideas were ignored, but when repeated by Ken, they were embraced enthusiastically.

Jen and her female colleagues experienced what many women face daily: difficulty in being heard and in participating in decision-making compared to male colleagues. While scholars debate the reasons for this, the phenomenon itself is well documented (Harris & Gonzalez, 2012). In some cases, women are not heard because they may not speak as much. At the same time, the vignette shared above points to another aspect of women in leadership: women bring unique and highly valuable skills and perspectives to leadership roles. Notably, Ken himself did not see the privilege that his voice received, but Jen, his female colleague, *did* and she worked with him to validate her observations. Jen and Ken did eventually share their "experiment" with the rest of the people sitting around that table, most of whom were women. When Jen revealed her analysis of her speaking experience in comparison to her male colleagues, she was met with shock, followed quickly by regret. The other teachers resolved to do better and to be more reflective about assigning cultural capital (power, weight, significance) to a person's speech based upon dominant identity markers. Jen's sense of activism is not uncommon among women leaders.

Women in leadership roles are often more likely to take on women's issues (Martin, 2011b), other issues of marginality (Gutierrez y Muhs et al., 2012) and to bring perspectives unique to women to light.

In this chapter, we first review the enduring challenges that women face in attaining positions of status and leadership and the theories that underpin these challenges. We then address the issues of differential expectations for leaders based upon biological sex, the issue of the underrepresentation of women leaders in education and the potential reasons for this, and the unique experiences women, including those of multiple minority status, face when they strive for or attain positions of leadership. Personal vignettes written by the authors will be interspersed throughout the chapter. We also offer the voices of a cadre of women holding leadership positions in K-12 education, as a way to elucidate and provide context to the literature.

Grounding the Paucity of Women's Leadership

Attribution Error

According to attribution theory, the personality characteristics (and personal accomplishments) of women and men are often perceived differently (Kirchmeyer, 1998). For example, women's accomplishments may be attributed to luck or other external factors; additionally, women's advancement may be attributed to affirmative action and not to personal ability (Kirchmeyer, 1998; Lyness & Thompson, 1997). Moreover, a woman's performance (on tasks traditionally perceived to be associated with male characteristics) is often attributed to luck or to effort, and men's performance is attributed to skill (Greenhaus & Parasuraman, 1993). The reason for the former can be explained through the idea that such successes violate people's sex role expectations; to avoid cognitive dissonance, many observers attribute negative attributes to women, such that women are not responsible for their own successes—they just "got lucky."

Vignette Two: Enduring Challenges for Women, a Student in My Office

One day, about halfway through the semester of teaching Multicultural Education, a student entered my office. Because I had previously taught this student in an Introduction to Education course, I felt very comfortable and open with this student. I motioned for him to enter my office and to sit down even though I had an Information Technology person assisting me with my computer at the time. As we were working on my computer, the student proceeded to tell me how he felt my course was "sexist" and made him feel angry. I asked him to name what I had done or said that was sexist, and he replied that he could not name an example, but he felt entitled enough, in front of another person that he did not know, to inform me that somehow I was not doing my job correctly. I wondered if he would have felt as comfortable speaking in a similar manner to a male professor, especially with someone else in the room.

Despite my shock and embarrassment at the situation, I attempted to defend my curriculum and my point of view. I attempted to inform him that because I broach the topic of sexism, this does not mean that I am sexist. It was as though he was attempting to shoot the messenger for suggesting that he think about things he had never before been asked to think about: his privilege. He did not like it, and he was looking for someone to blame.

It is not abundantly clear exactly why the student in the above vignette acted in this manner. Did he attribute his professor's position to some external factor, thus deeming her less than qualified for her position as authority figure in the classroom? Women in positions of leadership and authority, such as teachers and professors, may find it more difficult to be taken seriously in comparison with their male peers because of students' attribution errors, whether these errors are made explicit through overt resistance, or kept implicit, revealing themselves on course evaluations (Hamermesh & Parker, 2005; Toombs, 2013). Although we are committed to social justice pedagogy, we understand that not only is achieving tenure more difficult for women and faculty of color because of organizational cultures that do not support their work or their identities (Gutierrez y Muhs, et al. 2012; Jones, Taylor, & Coward, 2013), but also because this work is further complicated for those teaching courses with "unsafe content." According to Ludlow, Rodgers, and Wrighton (2005), "… resistant White/male heterosexual/mainstream students respond to diversity courses by inverting the dominant/subordinate paradigm: the White student perceives himself/herself to be subordinated by the discourse of diversity and resists it as if she/he were the marginalized group" (p. 8). In these instances, if the instructor holds a dominant identity status, she/he is less likely to face student resistance on evaluations. Conversely, the more distant the instructor's identity is from the dominant status, the more intensive, abusive, and discrediting the resistance can become (Ludlow et al., 2005, p. 8). In Vignette Two, the (dominant status) student felt entirely comfortable challenging this professor's curriculum in front of a stranger. Given these realities, engaging in social justice pedagogy and scholarship is not among the best advice for new faculty members seeking tenure (Patton, Shahjahan, & Osei-Kofi, 2010).

We are aware that professors who violate students' expectations, for instance, by asking them to move beyond their proscribed gender role expectations can face consequences (Bachen, McLoughlin, & Garcia, 1999); however, women tend to receive more negative repercussions for said approaches (Takiff, Sanchez, & Stewart, 2001). Experiencing gendered microaggressions—one of the enduring challenges women face, such as those mentioned above—can make it more difficult for women to become leaders, and for women to be taken seriously as leaders (Martin, 2011b).

Despite decades of feminist progress, women leaders still have to think about how they are perceived based upon the gender stereotypes held by others. According to Takiff et al. (2001), "Female professors, like other women in the workplace, may often have to decide whether to conform to traditional gender-role norms or to demand the status and success they deserve at the cost of likability" (p. 143). It is not uncommon for students to expect a maternal figure in their female professors, someone who is perpetually nice: someone who is not too challenging, someone who does not ask too many questions, for, as Sandler (1991) reminds us, gender can impact how students evaluate a faculty member's competence. According to Baker and Copp (1997), "… students may hold contradictory and unrealistic expectations of them [women]. These contradictions may make it hard for women faculty members to receive outstanding teaching evaluations, because students judge women by their gender performance" (p. 29). Attribution plays a part here too, as women's successes are often attributed to luck, while men's success is attributed to talent (Sandler, 1991).

Personal Agency and Gender Norms

The terms "agency" and "communion" were originally developed by Bakan (1966) to reflect two fundamental aspects of human existence. Agency describes a person's existence as an individual; communion describes a person's participation in a larger whole of which they belong. Bakan essentialized these constructs by attributing them to gender: agency as the male principle, communion as the female. Historically, women have tended to possess fewer agentic traits (or self-directed/self-promoting actions) than men (Eagly & Steffen, 1984). One reason for this involves the perceptions of observers, or the societal double bind. For example, when women take career risks or achieve success in nontraditional realms they may be viewed negatively by others. The same self-promoting actions in men (assertiveness) are often looked at as negative in women and are often subsequently relabeled (aggressiveness). "Aggressiveness" may include asking for a raise, a move fraught with risks for women. In essence, self-promotion in women may not be a "safe" course of action. Although some women leaders can withstand the negative labels of "bitchy" or "bossy," others find the cost too great: the risks involved becoming a leader in a field where women leaders are scarce are too personally taxing.

Additionally, because there are fewer women in positions of leadership, some may perceive women to be less capable of such positions; in other words, these ideas can translate to negative perceptions of women's capabilities (Eagly & Steffen, 1984)—which further leads to women's perceptions of their own capabilities (contributing to the vicious cycle which produces fewer women leaders). Women's acknowledgement of these negative perceptions of women leaders within the larger social construct can contribute to stereotype threat, causing their performance to weaken (Steele, 1997). In other words, when women feel responsible to represent their entire sex, or to alter the negative expectations and stereotypes placed upon their group, in areas where they represent the "one" or where they are in a minority, they may collapse under the pressure. Additionally, if women perceive their opportunities to be less than those of men, they may seek to strive for less or not seek promotions or leadership positions for fear of failure. This fear may cause a lack of motivation and thus perpetuate the cycle of few women in top management positions (Dreher, 2003).

Whiston and Bouwkamp (2003) found that career-oriented women are motivated by more intrinsic needs such as independence and achievement. This effect is directly associated with cultural expectations of women's work and acceptance of non-stereotypical gender roles. For example, Twenge (1997) found that while over time, communal traits have remained higher in women than in men, agentic traits have increased in women over time, as a result of the social re-framing of women's work and subsequent women's role performance. Accordingly, Twenge found that as the gap between women and men is decreasing in terms of feelings of personal agency, assertiveness (an agentic trait) in women has been increasing: a performance that varies with status and role. According to Abele (2003), both women and men displayed agentic or dominant traits when in positions of supervision; however, women presented as more communal (or submissive behaviors) when in positions of workplace subordination. Interestingly, women possessing non-majority identity status are oftentimes taught to internalize agentic traits as manifestations of their minority gendered selves. African American women, for example, are socialized into the Strong Black Woman (SBW) role (Sharp-Grier, 2013) and are expected, as part of their subcultural contextual identity as women, to be both agentic and communal as contextualized by the setting. This identity, because it does not represent the normed expectation of femininity, presents unique challenges to African American women leaders as they navigate what to them is culture shock, and to others, aggressive womanhood, within the professional milieu.

Vignette Three: Developing and Negotiating Leadership as a Non-majority Woman

Student organizations provide unique opportunities for young persons to develop the skills and acumen necessary to successfully enter into and succeed within professional and corporate venues. For Black women, opportunities to do so are often limited and present difficult hurdles. Tina, an African American assistant professor, assumed the leadership of an organization of Black women students. When she took on the role as advisor to the club, she knew that it was laden with issues that rendered the club fractured and ineffective. It was hemorrhaging membership, and the source of the flow was the president. Tina called the president of the org into her office to get to know her a bit, and to determine what she believed her role to be, as the ambassador of the organization. When the president arrived, Tina greeted her and started the conversation with pleasantries and an overview of why the meeting was called. When the president began discussing her leadership style, her demeanor changed—she became almost hostile and overtly demonstrative in a way that positioned herself not as a co-collaborator and leader of the group; rather she saw herself as an authoritarian figure, there to manage and control the members. Tina was struck by the president's posturing, but realized that her standpoint was not reflective of her desire to be dictatorial. Instead, she was attempting to juxtapose her perception of self as an African American, woman, leader—something about which she received conflicting social definitions, and for which she had not been provided mentoring.

In sum, self-actualized, secure, and independent women are not actively nurtured and cultivated by our society. There are still consequences for women who do not fit their prescribed role, including social ostracism and receiving negative personal feedback (Heilman, Wallen, Fuchs, & Tamkins, 2004). Career-oriented women and women leaders can be viewed by others as cold, bitter, quarrelsome, and selfish, when simply possessing the same personality characteristics as their male counterparts (Heilman et al., 2004). Women who behave in ways perceived as traditionally male are less well received than are men who deviate from traditional norms (Heilman et al., 2004). Sometimes it is subordinates' belief of personality characteristics as opposed to one's actual personality characteristics that pose the real problem for women leaders.

Evaluation of Women Leaders

Women's performance, credentials, and workplace outcomes, when they mirror men's, are not evaluated in a fashion similar to men's. This reality may partially explain why women do not have equitable access to positions of leadership; as previously stated, leadership qualities, such as assertiveness, may be viewed less favorably when exhibited by a woman (Eagly, Makhijani, & Klonsky, 1992). Eagly et al. (1992) found that women leaders were devalued in comparison with male leaders, when the leadership was carried out in a stereotypically masculine manner. This devaluation was exacerbated when women leaders occupied male-dominated realms and when male evaluators were used. Eagly et al. (1992) also found that women leaders were more harshly evaluated when they were evaluated by men, "Because placing women in leadership positions upsets the traditional societal gender hierarchy, male subjects might, in a sense, have more to lose by approving female leadership because their status vis-à-vis women would decline. Thus, male subjects may be more prone than female subjects to reject female leaders" (p. 7). Although the Eagly et al. study is more than 20 years old, not much has changed in terms of how people perceive and judge the qualities women leaders possess. As the following vignette will illustrate, it is not only men who are guilty of maligning women leaders for acting outside of traditional gender role expectations; women also can internalize sexism and use it to indict other women.

Vignette Four: "You're Abrasive!"

I chair the faculty committee on diversity initiatives on my campus. Although this committee is part of our system of faculty governance, additional members of the committee include student affairs staff members as well as students representing the various diversity organizations on campus. At our most recent meeting, we had invited the Vice President of Marketing to attend, so that she could hear students' concerns about diversity representation on the university's new website. After the students presented their concerns, a staff member new to the university, Susan,[1] *began detailing her own personal problems with the website, including the fact that her picture and personal bio were not yet online. I attempted to steer the conversation back to our agenda and to respect the schedule of the marketing representative, who had another engagement to attend. Because Susan's concerns were not in the purview of marketing, I asked that the Dean of Diversity and Inclusion (who was in attendance) update the personal information of the staff members in their office and to send it to marketing. However, Susan continued perseverating on her incredulity that she did not exist on the website. I could tell that she was hurt, but this was not a venting session. I stated, as gently as I could, "Susan, I am sorry, but I have to stop you there. We have to get back to the agenda and the Vice President needs to get to another… ." Before I could finish my sentence, she interrupted with, "You're abrasive!" I was shocked. I was sure that I had not heard correctly. I said, "What?" She replied, "We'll talk about it later. I was talking." Although perhaps I should not have been shocked, I was. I knew that being called "abrasive" in a meeting that is under my charge, and in front of students, is absolutely unacceptable. A gendered attack such as this on a committee charged with fostering diversity on campus is more than a little ironic. Instead of "speaking to me later," Susan stormed out of the meeting, long before the adjournment, soon after the VP of Marketing took her leave.*

Perhaps the author of the above vignette was not perceived as being sufficiently "nice." Would a man who engaged in the same behaviors be deemed as "abrasive?" Perceptions of personality characteristics aside, women also report that their styles of leadership are also obstacles to their advancement (Shinew & Arnold, 1998). Some women leaders describe their leadership styles as being fundamentally different from men. For example, women often attempt to get their subordinates to come to a consensus with the goal of the group. In general, however, the perception of how leadership should be conducted philosophically is still viewed in terms of individualistic traits (as opposed to relational traits) (Vinnicombe & Harris, 2000). Vinnicombe and Harris (2000) argue that this perception persists because of the processes (such as hidden attitudes and stereotypes) of the informal organization, "The balance of the sexes in management can still be summed up by the phrase 'think manager, think male,' just as it was in the 1970s" (p. 28). Should the author of the above vignette have allowed the extraneous discussion to continue because of the expectation that women are more relational? The problem is that socially, women are not provided access to a full gamut of personality characteristics and leadership styles. Women possessing "feminine" leadership styles may have their style questioned; for example, some women have their sense of calm misperceived as weakness (Williamson & Hudson, 2001). Women in positions of leadership, possessing a traditionally "feminine" style are often perceived as weak, wimpy, and wishy-washy (Williamson & Hudson, 2001). If women are direct, they are viewed as oppositional; if they are relational, they may be viewed as weak. Because women leaders are still the few, they remain the judged, especially when it comes to performance evaluation.

---

[1] A pseudonym.

Effective performance is often attributed to ability when the employee being observed is a member of the "in-group," as opposed to the token or out-group; in the latter case, success is often attributed to luck (Greenhaus & Parasuraman, 1993). This does not just apply to gender; it also applies to other nondominant statuses (Greenhaus & Parasuraman, 1993). Employees who were thought to perform well because of ability were also judged more worthy of promotions than were those whose successes were attributed to luck or effort (Greenhaus & Parasuraman, 1993). African American workers are subject to having their successes judged as not the logical outcome of the application of their talents and drive; but, rather as a vestige of affirmative action policies, which are erroneously perceived to include a mandatory "quota system," whereby organizations are required to hire and promote concrete numbers of Blacks, women, and other minorities to avoid federal scrutiny (Foster, 2015). Such perceptions are not only inaccurate, they also harm minority and women employees in that they discount the talents and abilities of the individuals scrutinized—suggesting that they were not hired because of *who* they are; rather, they were hired because of *what* they are (Exum, 1983). In short, they perpetuate the stereotype that "black folk just ain't smart" (Sharp-Grier, 2015). For Black women, in this instance, their intersectional selves—the nexus of their race, culture, and sex (Crenshaw, 1989) creates a unique path through which their expertise, performance, and outcomes may be evaluated.

Women experience discriminatory evaluation procedures, have their competence denied, and their performance devalued as a result of their sex (Heilman et al., 2004). These unfair processes perpetuate negative expectations for women. These negative expectations result from the inconsistency in how women are viewed and what characteristics are necessary to perform a particular job. Even when women are successful in traditionally male occupations, they may still be judged unfairly.

Unique Challenges for Women of Color

Reliable, self-sacrificing, gutsy, redeemer, fierce guardian, observer, attendant, partner, unstinting, supporter, rescuer (Parks, 2010). These words have been used to describe Black women, and to define their role in the social realm. It can be deduced from this list that the expectations of Black women are many, and in some ways, daunting. Parks, in *Fierce Angels: The Strong Black Woman in American Life and Culture* (2010), noted that this list is "humanly impossible" to achieve, yet is expected by both black culture and the dominant milieu. Woods-Giscombe (2010), in her analysis of stress-related outcomes of the Strong Black Woman (SBW) (Sharp-Grier, 2013) role, noted a "Superwoman Schema"—a set of variables with which the analysis of the SBW can be examined. She identified a multifaceted system of characteristics, contextual factors, benefits, and liabilities related to the SBW role, including individualities, which incorporate a manifestation of strength, an obligation to suppress emotion, a resistance to being vulnerable/dependent, a strong drive to succeed, and an obligation to help others (2010).

These traits have been normalized and incorporated into the interactive social milieu as a racial and gendered emotional prescription for Black women and are in direct opposition to what has been hegemonically presented as the ideal feminine display. This prescription has influenced not only the social understandings of Black women and subsequent responses to them (Sharp-Grier, 2013, 2015), they have also been adopted by the various institutions within which Black women in general, and Black women leaders, in particular, must navigate themselves. Parker and Ogilvie (1996) suggest that these socialized traits correlate directly to a distinctively African American female style of leadership, which recognizes the hegemonic White male model of understood "female" styles, but by nature of the internalized understanding of self as Black women, is more agentic, and must be enacted within the context of racial and gender discrimination. Because of what Alston (2000) suggests is a dearth of Black women school administrators, the African American woman's experience in leadership is oftentimes discounted and/or overlooked. Yet, it is a salient and tangible aspect of how Black women in leadership positions exact their work, and are subsequently evaluated by their peers—even in the classroom setting. This model is also complicit in manifesting outcomes of stress, uncertainty, and a plethora of physical and psychological responses to its adaptation.

Woods-Giscombe, in her 2010 work investigating how the "Superwoman Schema" affects the physical and mental health of Black women, noted that Black women are chronically exposed to psychological stress, which leads to cardiovascular, immune, and neuroendocrine problems. Parks (2010) noted that despite Black women undertaking *more* preventative health measures than other women, particularly regarding stress-related illnesses (heart disease, hypertension, obesity), they are more often afflicted with these maladies and die sooner than their counterparts. She explains that the "cultural lockdown" of the SBW: images and actions required by the Black community, and expected by the White, have led to this phenomenon.

Power and Influence

Women of color were found to have less influence within their departments than were White women. Women within the science field experience fewer opportunities for leadership and influence, slower advancement, heightened isolation, and the like. Settles, Cortina, Malley, and Stewart (2006) argue that in order for women to be successful in science-related fields, they must realize these three outcomes: job satisfaction, productivity, and "felt influence." Sexual harassment and sexist environments in general affect these areas (Paludi & Coates, 2011). These factors and the tolerance of them within the organization hinder the success of women and are tied to lower productivity and career outcomes for women (Settles et al., 2006).

As illuminated in vignette one, women can also hold sexist stereotypes. In a randomized double-blind study of 127 science faculty members at research universities, Moss-Racusin and colleagues (2012) found that faculty members rated identical application materials for a lab manager position of male applicants higher than female applicants. This bias in favor of male applicants was true for both male and female faculty. At the same time, we must note that women can also take the lead in identifying such biases, just as Jen did.

Sex stereotypes still exist and thus create a double standard that negatively affects the evaluations of women in management (Dreher, 2003; Pardine, Fox, & Salzano, 1995). The percentage of women in positions of management has increased since the mid-seventies; however, the perceptions still endure that women are unqualified or unable to perform in such capacities. Those women who do make it into positions of management do little to contribute to the change in perception or changes in stereotypes of women; on the contrary, these women are instead thought to be the "exception" to the stereotype (Pardine et al., 1995). They are thought to be unrepresentative of women in general—their accomplishments do not impact societal beliefs about the qualifications of women in positions of management (Pardine et al., 1995).

According to the American Association of University Professors 2006 equity study, women hold only 24% of full professor positions in the United States. Despite the gains women have made in higher education over the past few decades, they are highly underrepresented in tenure-track positions. Women in higher education face more obstacles to career advancement than in the corporate world (West & Curtis, 2006). The areas with the fewest number of women in higher education are the most prestigious and most highly paid. Women make far less than men in higher education because they are more likely to hold positions at institutions that pay lower salaries and they are less likely to gain senior rank.

In a meta-analysis of 45 studies, Eagly, Johannesen-Schmidt, and Van Engen (2003) found that women show more transformational leadership traits (such as charisma, inspirational motivation, intellectual stimulation, and individualize consideration) than men. Gupton and Slick (1996) argue that these traits are valuable, "Transformational leadership advocates participatory management that motivates others by transforming their self-interest into the goals of the organization. Transformational leaders are skilled in leadership patterns that inspire increased worker performance by encouraging all points of view" (p. 108). Transformational leadership necessitates relational leadership and values mentoring and the communal; it can establish a sense of connection between people. Transformational leadership is a non-hierarchical, non-patriarchal form of leading where the named leader shares the task of leading by utilizing the strengths of those in the organization. Decisions are made together and the tasks of leaders are shared. In fact, the most effective style of leadership is transformational leadership, which builds empowerment in a mutual and collaborative context (Eagly et al., 2003; Eagly, Karau, & Makhijani, 1995). Women most often utilize the transformational leadership style, a style that requires empathy and a sense of caring for others. Although research suggests that it is the most effective style of leadership, we have a paucity of women at the highest levels of leadership in most fields (West & Curtis, 2006; Dreher, 2003; Hopkins, O'Neil, Passarelli, & Bilimoria, 2008; White House Project, 2009). Additionally, transformational leaders often put their own self-interest in check for the good of the organization, as the following vignette will illustrate.

Vignette Four: "You're Abrasive!" Part II

In my view, sometimes leaders have to "take the hit" to protect their people or to serve the greater good; they put their personal feelings to the side for the overall benefit of the organization. Although I was very upset at being called "abrasive," I thought that perhaps the comment was not so much about me, but about Susan feeling virtually anonymous. I took a conciliatory approach by sending her the following email, "Thank you again for attending today's meeting. I fully understand your need to express your views about the website. That being said, ________ had already spent more time than she had allotted, as she expressed the need to get to another engagement prior to your arrival at the meeting. While trying to be respectful of __________'s time, I attempted to halt the conversation when it veered to topics not on our agenda and things not under her control. My apologies if I caused any discomfort on your part, for that was certainly not my intention. If you would like to address your concerns with me about the committee, or about any other issues, I would be happy to do so." However, I never got a reply. No response. No explanation for her behavior. No apology. Although I am not sure what the outcome of this situation will be, I am sure that as women leaders, we must be open about what we experience. To keep silent about the microaggressions we face will only compound their power upon us. And they do have power. Because this situation has not been resolved, I am anxious about the next meeting I will chair. But I will not keep silent. There is power in naming. And I name this as a gendered attack on my leadership.

Women leaders in K-12 leadership also face many challenges related to sex and race, and other minority statuses, as will be demonstrated later in the chapter.

Methods

Indigenous and feminist research methods are presented to voice the voiceless through the application of approaches most aligned with the narratives they seek to represent (Sharp-Grier & Martin, 2016). Such methodologies, when utilized as tools of decolonization, diminish the influence of the dominant voice, which has traditionally been employed to define and contextualize the lives and experiences of individuals possessing minority status in the current social milieu (Elabor-Idemudia, 2011), including women. Conventionally, research models have reflected the temporal and cultural standpoints of dominant groups. They have reflected and strengthened the predominant perspectives of the mythical norm (Lorde, 1997), which have at best reinforced stereotypical notions regarding social minority groups in general and at worst contributed to the dehumanization and infrahumanization of those persons (Goff, Jackson, Di Leone, Culotta, & DiTomasso, 2014; Sharp-Grier & Martin, 2016) and lessened life chances. According to Martin and Sharp-Grier (2016), "These approaches to social investigation have systematically framed minorities and women as other, and have viewed them as objects, rather than subjects of investigation. Their realities therefore have been interpreted and used by the majority without giving them voice to speak for themselves" (p. 58). As culture jamming scholars—those who utilize "… a form of communication, art, protest … which rejects the dominant cultural discourse regarding the marginalized…" (Sharp-Grier & Martin, 2016, p. 4), we endeavor to ensure that those with lived experiences are positioned as subjects rather than objects of analysis and are free to communicate their stories and to be provided the opportunity to disturb traditional research processes when said practices sublimate the recounting of lived experience. In so doing, in addition to outlining our analysis in empirical literature and adding our voices through autoethnographic narrative, we organized and conducted a focus group interview of seven women in K-12 leadership positions.

According to Warren and Karner (2005), because interviews have proven robust in producing abundant and illustrative accounts of empirical knowledge, we felt that such an approach would provide a full understanding of the firsthand experiences of women navigating leadership in educational venues. We conducted one focus group session during our investigation, which was held at a neutral location on the campus of a small Midwestern university. The participants represented three small- to mid-sized school districts. Two of the districts can be defined as urban, and one distinctly rural. The contributors ranged in age from 36 to 69 years of age. All but two held positions of Assistant Principal or higher within their school districts. Three of the seven identified as White, and four as Black or African American. Each provided pseudonyms for themselves, which will be utilized in the below-listed analysis to identify them. All seven women possessed a Master's degree, and two had earned their doctorates.

For the session, we composed and administered open-ended questions, which allowed the participants to speak to their unique experiences. As was expected in the group interview process, participants were free and willing to build on the discussions and responses of their colleagues, which yielded a conversational tone and collegial interaction. As Martin and Sharp-Grier (2016) state, "We developed our queries to evoke relaxed, 'inquisitive' dialogues, as opposed to 'investigative' exchanges. The discussions were guided, yet designed to encourage the free flow of information…" (p. 59). A similar approach was utilized in the current study, and ultimately resulted in the generation of a bond between the participants that carried beyond the confines of the focus group experience.

As implied above, we developed a very rough outline of questions, because we intended to allow participants to the discussion and allow it to move in the directions they deemed important. (The focus group questions can be found in Appendix). The interview lasted approximately 90 min and was recorded. It was later transcribed and coded for themes. In order to contain our own biases, we analyzed the data with the recognition that the group was one within which a strong reflexive process was generated. Recognizing reflexivity involves acknowledging the ways in which "our own agendas" impact our research at all points, including analysis and interpretation (Hesse-Biber, 2012, p. 17).

The acknowledgment necessitated that we examine and consider the impact of how our subjects' positions, locations, and beliefs impacted not only the interpretation of their own lived experience, but also that of their fellow cohort. Moreover, our recognition of the reflexive process similarly demanded that we, ourselves, consider our own biases, and how they impact what we choose to study, our motivations for the analysis, our methodological approach to study, and so on (Hesse-Biber, 2012). Continual member checking, informant feedback, and content validation, in order to ensure not only applicability but authenticity (Hesse-Biber, 2012) of information and interpretation, were practiced.

Data Analysis

We incorporated Saldana's (2016) method of *process coding* to analyze our data. Process coding involves highlighting gerunds within the data in order to connote observable and conceptual action. It is an action-oriented method. We selected this method based upon the tension women face between the active and passive gendered stereotypes of the leader. We thus wanted to determine if the women leaders spoke in an active or a passive voice, and if their style of voice conformed to their narrative telling.

This methodological process, active coding, encompassed several stages. We first conducted first cycle coding, recording all gerunds and the frequency of their occurrence. We then, as Saldana suggests, attempted to embody the process codes (to symbolically represent them physically) to get a sense of the overall understanding of conceptual action of the group as a whole.

Second, we developed a list of the most prominent process codes and engaged in other round of bode embodiment to get another sense of the overall understanding of the most prominent conceptual actions of the group. Through this process we developed common themes. Third, we reviewed the data and highlighted any key quotations that were paradigmatic of any of these themes.

Finally, we then had Chloe, our research assistant, scour through the narrative transcript and record her reactions. The first two authors, Martin and Sharp-Grier, then reanalyzed the data.

Results

Through the analysis of data, if a process code was only used once, it was removed from the gerund list, as we were looking for prominent and common actions. The four most prominent codes were "going [to]," "being," looking/watching," and "mentoring." Through the process of code embodiment, we realized that the process codes involved more of an aspirational symbolic conversation than a reporting of accomplishments. That is, the codes indicated to us that the women in the focus group talked much about what they were going to do, how they were perceived by others, what they observed in others and how they were observed, and their lack of and need for mentoring.

The prominent themes that we identified from the data were:

- Finding and giving voice (including feeling like an imposter)
- Differential expectations based on gender
- Mentoring and lack thereof
- Racialized and gendered microaggressions

These themes are not at all surprising and are in line with previous research. In sum, the women participating in the focus group lacked mentors, were one of the "only" of their identity markers in a position of leadership, and faced differential expectations and microaggressions based on their minority/multiple minority status(es) because of this.

Chloe's Analysis

The first conclusion I found through the focus group was all of the women had a hard time finding their voices, not only in their leadership roles, but in their daily lives. Participants suggested that it is often just easier to take on extra work, ignore comments made by their male counterparts, or to go about a situation by being funny, rather than just saying what is really on their minds or fighting. I also found that the four women of color found it even harder to speak their voice, even in the focus group. The three White women spoke 79 comments throughout the time of the group, whereas the four women of color only made 58 comments. I am not sure if this has to do with personality or race, but through the data the minority women spoke less.

Another large issue that came from the discussion was the role of family and child-rearing. Most of the women in the group had children, and they talked about the hardships of being in a role of leadership and also being a mother. One woman talked about the comparison between she and her male counterpart, both of whom had children around the same time. No one said anything to the man after the birth of his child, but for the woman, comments were made such as: "I could never leave my baby at home, how are you doing this, you know isn't it time for you to go home?" She reported that those comments have never been made to a man. Moreover, these comments were made by women. Another woman told about how her family resented her for continuing her education, and for arriving home or to her children's games late from work. Comments were made to her that she should stop her education, and her name would never change to her family members. And another woman said how she was the breadwinner in her family, so her husband took care of the children. It was not the role he wanted to play, which then created stress in their relationship.

Through listening to the women talk about their success and families, it seemed that the higher their success, the lower (status) their families and some counterparts saw them. In today's society women are still seen as wives and mothers, even if they are highly qualified for a position in leadership. It is as though these women have to carry the weight of their families and they must try to get their support. These women are not being supported or respected by their families, let alone as leaders.

Mentorship was a huge aspect throughout the discussion. Many of the women felt that they did not have proper mentors, and if they did then they all got too busy (and the mentorship dissolved). The question was asked, "How many women actually embrace other women, and offer mentorship?" The women stated that there was a lack of female role models. One woman stated that she felt as though people above her didn't want her to achieve. Many of the other women felt the same, and they wished they had support from other women leaders. The overall conclusion from the discussion was that women in these positions were busy, but they did need mentorship from others. These women felt that they needed more guidance, and wanted someone to talk to about these issues in educational leadership. No matter the age, experience, or educational background, these women in leadership had the desire to feel supported and have guidance from the others around them, yet it was hard to find.

The women also spoke of the microaggressions that they faced in their roles. Some of the women stated that men would be called by their title, while they were called by their first names. That could be another cause for these women feeling voiceless. Women in these higher positions have the same, if not more, training than their male counterparts; yet, they are not recognized as such. Other women stated how they had been called aggressive and a bitch, while the men (with similar traits) are called great leaders. One woman shared how a parent had called the school and asked for the "black principal." Statements like this are meant to tear women in leadership down. These words take away from the success and make the woman seem average and unimportant.

Overall, the results of the focus group were encouraging, in that the women shared their similar experiences and talked about how they could mentor one another. The conversation also showed that women in leadership must work harder than men to succeed. Once a woman does succeed and gets into a powerful position, the others around her still see her as just a female, wife, and mother. Women of color have these issues plus having to navigate race in the situation, so they then become the "black principal," rather than just the principal. Through the focus group, the comments made mostly focused on issues from: feeling voiceless, family and educational issues, needing more women mentors, and microaggressions. Although these are not the only issues women in leadership face, these are some of the most prominent issues suggested by the conversations in the focus group.

Thematic Analysis

The prominent themes that we identified from the data were: finding and giving voice (including feeling like an imposter), differential expectations based on gender, mentoring and lack thereof, and racialized and gendered microaggressions.

Our first theme, finding and giving voice (including feeling like an imposter), we found most prominently within the African American participants in the focus group:

> I have the same obstacle feeling like your voice is silent.... I'm gonna say that I thought my voice was silenced on multiple occasions. I'm gonna say even getting into the field during an interview process, this before I got the job, another time. They looked at my resume and your resume looked excellent, in fact it looks like you've done too much. What types of things do you do for fun? They said this—I was told—I'm going to ask this question, it hasn't been asked to anybody else, but what types of things do you do for fun? I'm confused. Am I qualified for this based off of the things I have listed on my resume?—Naomi, African American, 44 years old

Naomi's sentiments represent the classic double bind of what individuals possessing minority statuses face. They feel like imposters so they try to achieve more than their majority status peers, to be considered half as good. It is a "damned if you do, damned if you don't" situation.

Our second theme, differential expectations based on gender, ran the gamut from additional workload (inequitable division of labor based on gender) and being asked to take care of all "kin keeping" tasks. For example:

> When gifts needed to be bought and thoughtful things needed to be done, when caring type activities needed to be done, but what was also very strange—I don't know if any of you have any experience with this—but whenever there was really a crisis situation, I often would turn around and everybody was gone and I was the one. And so we started this foxhole I would say well, I will tell people to say are you in my foxhole? You will not be in my foxhole, because I noticed that the men, when it was like a conflict situation that required personal skill they would just kinda back up. And that's been a trend. I don't know.... And it's been all the way through my career—Scout, White, 56 years old

Scout speaks to the fact that she was often left alone to deal with problems. Another differential expectation was that of child-rearing.

Emma speaks to the fact that her male colleague had an easier time than did she with having and raising children while working. Emma received negative judgments for returning to work soon after having a child, although the primary breadwinner in her family:

> I can speak to that, my predecessor and I had almost the exact same experience in the past two years. And that was in terms of expanding our families. My predecessor had his first child during his tenure I had my baby this year as well. And while it was tough, I feel I weathered the storm pretty well. But I just noticed how often people had said, 'I could never leave my baby that soon. How are you doing this? You know isn't it time for you to go home? You need to go home.' I often find myself saying, you would had never said this to him.—Emma, African American, 36 years old

At the time of this writing, 2016, women still experience negative feedback for holding the dual roles of leader and mother.

Our third theme, mentoring and lack thereof, speaks to the fact that *all* of the women who participated in our focus group lacked mentors during their aspirational period when attempting to attain leadership roles, and in their current roles as leaders:

> I feel like I'm always looking for affirmation, looking for the nod like okay. Looking for that yep you're doing it. You're fine, you're doing a good job from colleagues and just everywhere I just- in my personal life too, because I feel so guilty.—Holly, White, 47 years old

Although some were mentored by male colleagues and bosses, all lacked other women as mentors and desired to keep talking about their experiences within the focus group. We titled our paper, "The Focus Group becomes the Support Group," because the women desired to keep the conversation going, resulting in a "Group Me" group text application where they could continue to support one another, and the communal desire to meet regularly with the researchers to continue the talk and support one another. Holly provided an insightful sentiment about the loneliness and sense of rejection she felt as the lone woman working in a central office leadership position:

> How am I going to be able to survive?—Holly, White, 47 years old

Our fourth theme, racialized and gendered microaggressions, was perhaps the most salient in our analysis. Emma and Janae both reported being victims of racialized attacks, and Janae reported a racialized and gendered attack when she is called a "Black Bitch."

> I had a parent call and said, "Let me talk to that black principal." And so when I answered the phone I said, "This is the black principal. What do you need from the black principal? The black principal is here." I just kept repeating it over and over again until they understood, you know without saying anything negative. I had to let them know, this is the black principal.—Emma, African American, 36 years old

Emma, being a very direct leader, subtly let this parent know that this language was unacceptable, and this worked for her. Janae, on the other hand, was still processing her own attack, which she attempted to characterize as a "double whammy":

> I think being called a black b is pretty upsetting, so that's worse than just being called a b 'cause there's a whole lot of other stuff that is implied with that and there are some signs that are very—that just right there, I don't handle that well. And so it happens and it's a double, I don't know what to call it….—Janae, African American, 52 years old

Janae did not reveal the specifics of her attack or her attacker. She did not even speak the entire phrase explicitly, but the pain and shock were evident on her face.

Another finding that stemmed from the racialized and gendered microaggressions theme was that of pay and recognition. That is, microaggressive comments from colleagues reveal inequities in pay and perceptions that women should not, or do not need to, get paid as much as men for the same work because they have husbands at home:

> Both formal and informal, just recognition. I was recently presented in a totally different context, the salaries, and the administrative salaries in our district and the treasurer, as soon as it was handed to me, she knew I had not seen it yet because I do not have a poker face. And I'm the assistant superintendent and you think I would know…So those, those, they still exist.—Holly, White, 47 years old

Additionally, microaggressive comments or microinvalidations reveal that women's work/women's leadership is not recognized or valued on equal terms with male peers. This causes the women in the focus group to reveal feelings of inadequacy, anger, and outrage:

> I just had a recent experience with that and I was really ticked off about it, not salary, but a comment was made about an opportunity that I was interested in and someone said, 'Oh

> you don't need the money.' And I… said, You know it isn't just racist, there is gender and you might not realize this, because in our district we talk about, you know racist issues a lot, and we don't talk about gender. And it was a male, [he] was clueless why that offended me. I said you would never say that to a man, you wouldn't. Never say that to a man.—Scout, White, 56 years old

Scout also shares an experience indicative of how women's leadership is not always respected by male colleagues:

> At the beginning of the school year in front of the entire staff I called out a male teacher, you know, 'Why do we have to do this, blah blah?' And it was very derogatory you some of the things which we spoke and everybody's looking at me, 'How's she going to deal with this?' And I've been in relationship, being proactive having a good relationship with your staff so that if you're ever have to be in a position, but I made a point as soon as the section was done I walked over to this man in front of everyone 'cause they all wanted to see it and you know we joked, he apologized, but I did not call him out right at that moment, that would not have been appropriate, but I made sure, I didn't walk around the perimeter I walked up the middle.—Scout, White, 56 years old

It is doubtful that similar behavior would have occurred had Scout been a male administrator.

It was very interesting to contrast the experiences of Emma, (African American, 36 years old) and Rue (White, 69 years old). Rue was a retired superintendent of a small rural district, and Emma is a current principal of an urban elementary school. Rue often spoke of, and advised the other women in the focus group to do the same, circumventing the exclusions she faced by "going around them," or "going through the back door," or "playing the game." She gave advice such as, "stand under the basketball hoop with your arms folded," when others felt that they were not taken seriously as women leaders. However, well-intended, her advice did nothing to trouble or to dismantle the institutional factors that impeded women, particularly women of color, and their success as leaders, many of whom were the first.

Emma, on the other hand, refused to play these games. As she states, "*I feel like I'm meant to be more of the aggressive person. I'm very private, and I don't do boys club thing.*" Emma, the primary breadwinner in her family, is a very direct person and deals with issues of justice and oppression in her school on a daily basis. "*Social justice is a huge issue,*" she stated.

Finally, it was interesting to note that most of the women in the focus group expressed the feeling that they were being surveilled:

> And people are watching you…I feel like I've been talking a lot. I don't care to, but one of the things that has been said to me over and over again and that I resent is, 'Don't let them see you cry.'—Holly, White, 47 years old

In sum, the women in the focus group felt as though their leadership was being scrutinized more so than their male counterparts.

Discussion and Conclusions

As alluded to previously, the women in the focus group did not want to leave the room when the allotted time was up. We, the researchers had planned for 1 h. We had to stop the group at the 90-min mark, but many women continued to talk and exchange contact information. We suggested that we schedule another group, whether or not to be used for the purposes of research, because of the urgent need for these women to talk and share their experiences. The women even suggested that we meet regularly, making it clear that this was a great need—they had never had the opportunity to have conversations with other women experiencing the very same issues and problems—that is was therapeutic for them. Thus, the focus group became for them a bit like a support group.

What surprised us about the focus group was how in line our participants' experiences were with previous research on women leaders in education; in fact, we were surprised that the situation has not improved much since such research began to be conducted decades ago. As described above, women still face numerous obstacles when it comes to attaining and maintaining positions of leadership.

Despite the aforementioned and continued struggles women face, Kropiewnicki and Shapiro (2001) identify strengths that female leaders bring to educational settings. They describe an ethic of care possessed by women administrators, prompting them to act in the best interest of others, to do what they felt was right for students, the school, teachers, and other stakeholders. The women in our study were motivated by self-possession, financial need, and sustained by outside support systems, such as friends and family. It is our hope that our participants will continue to find solace and support with our continued focus group, whether or not it be for the purposes of research.

The preceding also reinforced the socialization into and subsequent utilization by African American (AA) women of culturally sanctioned gender roles that revolve around emotional stoicism (Beauboeuf-Lafontant, 2005; Frame, Willams, & Green, 1999). The SBW is a reflection of these roles, and a disposition that older generations of AA women forged within their daughters as a method of ensuring their ability to navigate the social world (Beauboeuf-Lafontant, 2005). After all, women of color, specifically Black women, have historically had to be self-reliant and robust (Hill & Sprague, 1999; Rodriguez, 2006). They were the ones who have had to both "bring home the bacon and fry it up in the pan" for the sake of their families (Frame et al., 1999). Black women were taught to "do what you have to do," and not let on that they were hurting (Williams, 2008). In this regard, SBWs engage in emotion management to mask their true selves (Rodriguez, 2006), and pick up the mantle of "superwoman" in an attempt to effectively manage themselves and their environments (Williams, 2008). Emma's conveyance of her refusal to "play the game" that Rue suggested as a mechanism through which gender inequities could be navigated highlights the invocation of the SBW and the differential understanding of self within a leadership milieu for African-American women. Emma aptly articulated her deployment of the leadership style that Parker and Ogilvie (1996) suggested is the methodology through which Black women must both present self and be interpreted by others, so as to negate the microaggressive (and often macroaggressive) milieu within which they enact their role. This invocation of leadership is not only a method of identity presentation, it is representative of a level of emotion management that all women, but particularly Black women, must undertake.

Lively (2000) identified two types of emotion management: (a) individual (management of self) and (b) interpersonal (management of others). As part of the SBW persona, Black women engage in individual emotion management on a hypervigilant scale. They suppress and internalize not only feelings of frustration in dealing with others as members of a greater culture that views them as innately incapable and expects stereotypical behavior of them, but they also smother individual feelings of grief, exhaustion, sadness, and fear in order to maintain the impression of being emotionally stable and aloof (Beauboeuf-Lafontant, 2005). This maintenance of self-emotion is a function of feeling and display rules (Hochschild, 1983; Lively, 2000) relative to gender relations in the Black community. Black women are to maintain competence and stoicism in personal demeanor, and engage in caretaking (Beauboeuf-Lafontant, 2005; Lively, 2000).

The Black women in the group consistently reinforced notions of identity formation and renegotiation within the context of their leadership roles—they spoke of engaging in what Goffman (1959) identified as "facework." For Goffman, the idea that individuals conduct themselves in such a way that allows others to see only their desired attributes is embodied in this concept. For SBWs it is a way of life, and a style of leadership. SBWs are taught to manage their behavior, both towards self and others: they construct their own identity, and take active steps towards ensuring that others perceive their composed (pun intended) creed (Swann, 1987). They actively engage in what Cross, Strauss, and Fhagen-Smith (1999) identified as buffering: engaging in behaviors that provide self-defense against racism, thereby allowing self to control the immediate situation. Part of this buffering process is code-switching (Cross et al., 1999), or utilizing the language, posturing, and demeanor that reinforces the norms and regulations of the dominant group, including prescribed gender presentation. As noted, buffering, as enacted through behaviors such as code-switching, is reflective of not only identity regulation, but also emotion management, both of which provide African-American women leaders a modicum of protection against the bilateral realities of racism and sexism that pervade their work spaces.

The process of emotion management is not just one whereby SBWs maintain a positive affect in the face of diminished status and concurrent negative emotional display by others (Erickson & Ritter, 2001; Hochschild, 1983; Lively, 2000), it is also a mechanism whereby they fortify the SBW myth. It is a ritual of impression management that promotes dramaturgical loyalty (acceptance of and fidelity to the role of the SBW), dramaturgical discipline (suppression of emotion and self-control), and dramaturgical circumspection (adherence to the feeling rules associated with the role of the SBW) (Goffman, 1959; Harlow, 2003). In this context, instead of Black women's lower gender and social status being reinforced through emotion management, the unique presentation of self-sacrifice, stoicism, and strength (Beauboeuf-Lafontant, 2005, 2007; Woods-Giscombe, 2010) elevates their status from the submissive to the SBW.

Strategies and Suggestions

In our estimation, these issues reflect not only a general challenge regarding women and leadership in education, but a specific method of leadership that women must undertake, which must be addressed within the context of leadership training. Vinnicombe and Singh (2002), in their discussion of methodologies through which women leaders may obtain the skills and techniques to successfully navigate the management milieu, identified women-only leadership training and mentoring as a way to provide fledgling leaders the tools needed to enact leadership roles within the context of a male-dominated environment. The women in our focus group echoed the need for women to train and learn from each other, which reflects Vinnicombe and Singh's (2002) assertion that such preparation would be productive. We also suggest that both potential and practicing women managers and leaders be afforded women-only mentoring and training, not in place of traditional managerial training and education, but in addition to it. We have learned that this type of modeling can be immeasurably effective in fostering self-efficacy and subsequent performance of women in leadership. This may be particularly effective for nonminority women, who face unique challenges and barriers to their leadership.

One of our greatest takeaways from this research was the dilemma many women leaders in education face: that of "likeability versus authenticity." That is, many women leaders must decide whether they plan to "play the game," or to be their authentic selves and face the consequences. That is not to say that some women leaders cannot be exactly who they are *and* be liked. However, our research indicates that this usually is not the case. Women leaders may have to face the "likability" challenge that men do not have to face. That is, they may have to compromise and "play the game" in order to be "liked," and to be accepted. This is salient particularly for women of color, as indicated by Emma, who identified the unique role that her intersectional self (Crenshaw, 1989) played within the context of her leadership role. We suggest that a leadership training scheme as iterated by Vinnicombe and Singh (2002) would teach women—not just women of color—the skills to buffer (Cross et al., 1999) against hegemonic expectations of leadership.

Many other of the issues that women leaders face as revealed by our research are: women still face inequities regarding motherhood and child-rearing issues, women still lack mentoring, and women still face differential expectations based on sex. These issues are reflective of the cultured and gendered expectations associated with womanhood, and not unexpectedly, manifest in the general milieu.

Unfortunately, we do not have easy answers to the problems and issues that women leaders in education still face. We question whether easy solutions exist for the deep-rooted issues of sexism and racism. The lessons that the focus group taught us were to find mentors where you can and find support when and where you can. Do something to manage stress, and pay attention to self-care.

Appendix

Focus Group Questions

1. What made you aspire to become ____?
2. Were people in your field encouraging and supportive of your experiences?
3. What were your struggles to get where you are in your position today?
4. Have you ever experienced bias against you based on your sex, gender, race?
5. How do/have you deal/dealt with situations where you have experienced biased situations?
6. How do you advocate equity in your profession?
7. Have you ever had issues with people taking you seriously in your profession?
8. Do you feel more pressure than your male colleagues in your position?
9. Were you ever told you would be better in a different field/position?

Do you feel judge on your physical appearance more so than your male colleagues?

References

Abele, A. E. (2003). The dynamics of masculine-agentic feminine-communal traits: Findings from a prospective study. *Journal of Personality, 85*(4), 768–776.

Alston, J. A. (2000). Missing from action: Where are the black female school superintendents? *Urban Education, 35*(5), 525–531.

Bachen, C. M., McLoughlin, M. M., & Garcia, S. S. (1999, July). Assessing the role of gender in college students' evaluations of faculty. *Communication Education, 48*, 193–210.

Bakan, D. (1966). *The duality of human existence*. Chicago, IL: Rand McNally.

Baker, P., & Copp, M. (1997, January). Gender matters most: The interaction of gendered expectations, feminist course content, and pregnancy in student course evaluations. *Teaching Sociology, 25*, 29–43.

Beauboeuf-Lafontant, T. (2007). "You have to show strength": An exploration of gender, race, and depression. *Gender and Society, 2*(1), 28–51.

Beauboeuf-Lafontant, T. (2005). Keeping up appearances, getting fed up: The embodiment of strength among African American women. *Meridians: Feminism, Race, Transnationalism, 5*(2), 104–123.

Crenshaw, K. (1989). Demarginalizing the intersection of race and sex: A black feminist critique of antidiscrimination doctrine, feminist theory and antiracist politics. *University of Chicago Legal Forum, 140*, 139–167.

Cross, W. E., Strauss, L., & Fhagen-Smith, P. (1999). African American identity development across the life span: Educational implications. In R. H. Sheets & E. R. Hollins (Eds.), *Racial and ethnic identity in school practices: Aspects of human development* (pp. 29–47). Mahwah, NJ: Lawrence Erlbaum.

Dreher, G. F. (2003). Breaking the glass ceiling: The effects of sex ratios and work-life programs on female leadership at the top. *Human Relations, 56*(5), 541–562.

Eagly, A. H., Johannesen-Schmidt, M. C., & Van Engen, M. L. (2003). Transformational, transactional, and laissez-faire leadership styles: A meta-analysis comparing women and men. *Psychological Bulletin, 129*(4), 569–591.

Eagly, A. H., Karau, S. J., & Makhijani, M. G. (1995). Gender and the effectiveness of leaders: A meta-analysis. *Psychological Bulletin, 117*(1), 125–145.

Eagly, A. H., Makhijani, M. G., & Klonsky, B. G. (1992). Gender and the evaluation of leaders: A meta-analysis. *Psychological Bulletin, 111*(1), 3–22.

Eagly, A. H., & Steffen, V. J. (1984). Gender stereotypes stem from the distribution of women and men into social roles. *Journal of Personality and Social Psychology, 46*(4), 735–754.

Elabor-Idemudia, P. (2011). Identity, representation, and knowledge production. In C. A. Bowers (Ed.), *Counterpoints—Indigenous philosophies and critical education: A reader* (Vol. 379, pp. 142–156). New York, NY: Peter Lang.

Erickson, R. J., & Ritter, C. (2001). Emotional labor, burnout, and inauthenticity: Does gender matter? *Social Psychology Quarterly, 64*(2), 146–163.

Exum, W. H. (1983). Climbing the crystal stair: Values, affirmative action, and minority faculty. *Social Problems, 30*(4), 383–399.

Foster, J. C. (2015). David Hamilton Golland. constructing affirmative action: The struggle for equal employment opportunity. *Enterprise & Society, 16*(02), 464–466.

Frame, M. W., Willams, C. B., & Green, E. (1999). Balm in Gilead: Spiritual dimensions in counseling African American women. *Journal of Multicultural Counseling and Development, 27*(4), 192–193.

Goff, P. A., Jackson, M. C., Di Leone, B. A., Culotta, C. M., & DiTomasso, N. A. (2014). The essence of innocence: Consequences of dehumanizing black children. *Journal of Personality and Social Psychology, 106*(4), 526–545.

Goffman, E. (1959). *The presentation of self in every day life*. Gordon City, NY: Doubleday.

Greenhaus, J. H., & Parasuraman, S. (1993). Job performance attributions and career advancement prospects: An examination of gender and race effects. *Organizational Behavior and Human Decision Processes, 55*, 273–297.

Gupton, S. L., & Slick, G. A. (1996). *Highly successful women administrators: The inside stories of how they got there*. Thousand Oaks, CA: Corwin Press.

Gutierrez y Muhs, G., Flores Niemann, Y., Gonzalez, C. G., & Harris, A. P. (Eds.). (2012). *Presumed incompetent: The intersections of race and class for women in academia*. Boulder, CO: Utah State University Press.

Hamermesh, D. S., & Parker, A. (2005). Beauty in the classroom: Instructors' pulchritude and putative pedagogical productivity. *Economics of Education Review, 24*(4), 369–376.

Harlow, R. (2003). "*Race doesn't matter, but…*": The effect of race on professors' experiences and emotion management in the undergraduate college classroom. *Social Psychology Quarterly, 66*(4), 348–363.

Harris, A. P., & Gonzalez, C. G. (2012). Introduction. In G. Gutierrez y Muhs, Y. Flores Niemann, C. G. Gonzalez, & A. P. Harris (Eds.), *Presumed incompetent: The intersections of race and class for women in academia* (pp. 1–14). Boulder, CO: Utah State University Press.

Heilman, M. E., Wallen, A. S., Fuchs, D., & Tamkins, M. M. (2004). Penalties for success: Reactions to women who succeed at male gender-typed tasks. *Journal of Applied Psychology, 89*(3), 416–427.

Hill, S., & Sprague, J. (1999). Parenting in black and white families: The interaction of gender with race and class. *Gender and Society, 13*(40), 480–502.

Hochschild, A. R. (1983). *The managed heart*. Berkeley, CA: University of California Press.

Hopkins, M. M., O'Neil, D. A., Passarelli, A., & Bilimoria, D. (2008). Women's leadership development: Strategic practices for women and organizations. *Consulting Psychology Journal: Practice and Research, 60*(4), 348–365.

Jones, S. J., Taylor, C. M., & Coward, F. (2013). Through the looking glass: An autoethnographic view of the perceptions of race and institutional support in the tenure process. *The Qualitative Report, 18*(58), 1–16.

Kirchmeyer, C. (1998). Determinants of managerial career success: Evidence and explanation of male/female differences. *Journal of Management, 24*(6), 673–692.

Kropiewnicki, M. I., & Shapiro, J. P. (2001). *Female leadership and the ethic of care: Three case studies*. Paper presented at the annual meeting of the American Educational Research Association, Seattle, WA. April 10–14.

Lively, K. J. (2000). Reciprocal emotion management: Working together to maintain stratification in private law firms. *Work and Occupations, 27*(1), 32–63.

Lorde, A. (1997). Age, race, class, and sex: Women redefining difference. *Cultural Politics, 11*, 374–380.

Ludlow, J., Rodgers, L. A., & Wrighton, M. G. (2005). Students' perceptions of instructors' identities: Effects and interventions. *Academic Exchange Extra*. Retrieved May 20, 2014, from http://www.unco.edu/ae-extra/2005/3/Art-2.html.

Lyness, K. S., & Thompson, D. E. (1997). Above the glass ceiling? A comparison of matched samples of female and male executives. *Journal of Applied Psychology, 82*(3), 359–375.

Martin, J. L. (Ed.). (2011b). *Women as leaders in education: Succeeding despite inequity, discrimination, and other challenges. Volume 2: Women as leaders in classrooms and schools*. Santa Barbara, CA: Praeger.

Martin, J. L., & Sharp-Grier, M. L. (2016). Lest we forget, the personal continues to be political: Yik Yak and other unsafe spaces, necessary dialogue in a time of silence. In M. Paludi (Ed.), *Campus action against sexual assault: Needs, policies, procedures, and training programs* (pp. 51–82). Westport, CT: Praeger.

Moss-Racusin, C. A., Dovidio, J. F., Brescoll, V. L., Graham, M. J., & Handelsman, J. (2012). Science faculty's subtle gender biases favor male students. *Proceedings of the National Academy of Sciences of the United States of America, 109*(41), 16474–16479.

Paludi, M. A., & Coates, B. E. (Eds.). (2011). *Women as transformational leaders: From grassroots to global interests. Volume 2: Organizational obstacles and solutions*. Santa Barbara, CA: Praeger.

Pardine, P., Fox, I., & Salzano, J. (1995). *Substereotypes and requisite management characteristics*. Washington, DC: U.S. Department of Education. (Eric Document Reproduction Services. ED397239).

Parker, P. S., & Ogilvie, D. T. (1996). Gender, culture, and leadership: Toward a culturally distinct model of African-American women executives' leadership strategies. *The Leadership Quarterly, 7*(2), 189–214.

Parks, S. (2010). *Fierce angels: The strong Black Woman in American life and culture*. New York, NY: One World Press.

Patton, L. D., Shahjahan, R. A., & Osei-Kofi, N. (2010). Introduction to the emergent approaches to diversity and social justice in higher education special issue. *Equity & Excellence in Education, 43*(3), 265–278.

Rodriguez, D. (2006). Un/masking identity: Healing our wounded souls. *Qualitative Inquiry, 12*(6), 1067–1090.

Saldana, J. (2016). *The coding manual for qualitative researchers*. Los Angeles, CA: SAGE.

Sandler, B. R. (1991). Women faculty at work in the classroom, or, why it still hurts to be a woman in labor. *Communication Education, 40*, 1–15.

Settles, I. H., Cortina, L. M., Malley, J., & Stewart, A. J. (2006). The climate for women in academic science: The good, the bad, and the changeable. *Psychology of Women Quarterly, 30*, 47–58.

Sharp-Grier, M. (2013). *Ain't no pity party here!: African American women's socialization into the sbw*. Presented at the ninth international congress of qualitative inquiry. The University of Illinois, Champaign-Urbana, Champaign, IL.

Sharp-Grier, M. L. (2015). "She was more intelligent than I thought she'd be!": Status, stigma, and microaggressions in the academy. In J. Martin (Ed.), *Racial battle fatigue: Insights from the front lines of social justice advocacy*. Westport, CT: Praeger.

Sharp-Grier, M. L., & Martin, J. L. (2016). Broken windows, broken promises: Grief, privilege, and hope in the mythical post racial. A call and response. *Qualitative Inquiry, 22*, 561–567. https://doi.org/10.1177/1077800415624716.

Shinew, K. J., & Arnold, M. L. (1998). Gender equity in the leisure services field. *Journal of Leisure Research, 30*(2), 177–194.

Steele, C. M. (1997). A threat in the air: How stereotypes shape intellectual identity and performance. *American Psychologist, 52*(6), 613–629.

Swann, W. B., Jr. (1987). Identity negotiation: Where two roads meet. *Journal of Personality and Social Psychology, 53*(6), 1038–1051.

Takiff, H. A., Sanchez, D. T., & Stewart, T. L. (2001). What's in a name? The status implications of students' terms of address for male and female professors. *Psychology of Women Quarterly, 25*, 134–144.

Toombs, C. (2013). *Diverse faculty: The collision of academic freedom, course content/subject matter, student evaluations, student conduct, research areas, and colleagues*. Seattle, WA: AAUP Summer Institute.

Twenge, J. M. (1997). Changes in masculine and feminine traits over time: A meta-analysis. *Sex Roles, 36*, 305–325.

Vinnicombe, S., & Harris, H. (2000). A gender hidden. *People Management, 6*, 28–29.

Vinnicombe, S., & Singh, V. (2002). Women-only management training: An essential part of women's leadership development. *Journal of Change Management, 3*(4), 294–306.

Warren, C. A. B., & Karner, T. X. (2005). *Discovering qualitative methods: Field research, interviews, and analysis*. Los Angeles, CA: Roxbury Publishing.

West, M. S., & Curtis, J. W. (2006). *AAUP faculty gender equity indicators 2006*. Washington, DC: American Association of University Professors.

White House Project (2009). *Report: Benchmarking women's leadership*. Retrieved on February 10, 2018 from http://benchmarks.thewhitehouseproject.org.

Whiston, S. C., & Bouwkamp, J. C. (2003). Ethical implications of career assessment with women. *Journal of Career Assessment, 11*(1), 59–75.

Williams, T. (2008). *Black pain: It just looks like we're not hurting*. New York, NY: Scribner.

Williamson, R. D., & Hudson, M. B. (2001, April). *New rules for the game: How women leaders resist socialization to old norms*. Paper presented at the annual meeting of the American Educational Research Association, Seattle, WA.

Woods-Giscombe, C. L. (2010). Superwoman schema: African American women's views on stress, strength, and health. *Qualitative Health Research, 20*(5), 668–683.

Issues Confronting Women Leaders in Academia: The Quest for Equality Continues

Divya A. Patel, Gavin D. Sanders, Paula K. Lundberg-Love, John A. Gallien, and Cortni D. Smith

If you are successful, it is because somewhere, sometime, someone gave you a life or an idea that started you in the right direction. Remember also that you are indebted to life until you help some less fortunate person, just as you were helped.

Melinda Gates

Introduction

Women have surpassed men in attaining postsecondary degrees during the past few decades. In 1990, there was not a significant difference between the number of men and women aged 25–29 who earned their bachelor's degrees. However, by 2013, 37% of women of those ages had been awarded their bachelor's degrees as compared to only 30% of men, and 9% of women versus 6% of men had earned a master's degree or higher (Kena et al., 2014). Indeed, the number of women enrolled in post-baccalaureate programs has surpassed those of men since 1988 (Snyder & Dillow, 2015). For example, during 2000–2012, the enrollment of full-time female post-baccalaureate students rose by 42%, compared with a 28% increase in the number of their male counterparts (Snyder & Dillow, 2015). The number of women employed as professors in academia has also increased. In 1975, women accounted for approximately 25% of assistant professors, 17% of associate professors, and 10% of full professors (American Association of College and Universities [AACU], 2011). In 2004, these figures escalated to 50%, 38%, and 24%, respectively (AACU, 2011).

Despite this progress, however, discrimination against women continues in educational settings around the world and is particularly apparent when one examines the presence of women in higher level academic positions (Morley, 2006). Few women gain top-level positions in the higher educational system. Nidiffer (2010) addressed the fact

D. A. Patel (✉) · G. D. Sanders · P. K. Lundberg-Love · J. A. Gallien · C. D. Smith
University of Texas at Tyler, Tyler, TX, USA
e-mail: dpatel6@patriots.uttyler.edu

F. L. Denmark, M. A. Paludi (eds.), *Women and Leadership*,
https://doi.org/10.1007/978-3-319-72182-8_6

that while women equal men at the level of assistant professor, few advance to become full professors. Thornton (2010) reported that only one-third of full professorships were held by women. Furthermore, women faculty positions are highly underrepresented in the fields of science and engineering. The National Science Foundation (2008) reported that women comprised only 18% full professors in these areas. Additionally, women are also underrepresented in leadership roles in academia (Chin, 2011; Nidiffer, 2010). Women accounted for only 26.4% of university presidents (S. Cook, 2012b) and less than 30% of board members of colleges and universities (Lapovskey, 2009).

Traditionally in academia, women have held supportive administrative positions rather than actual positions of leadership. Indeed, they are more likely to be employed at a lower academic rank than their male counterparts (Snyder & Dillow, 2015). So the question emerges, why is there such a disparity between academic men and women with respect to leadership roles? Those that fill these positions attempt to justify their selections by claiming that there are few women who are qualified for the role. This theory is known as the "pipeline myth" (Eagly and Karau, 2002; Johnson, 2016). It is propagated despite the fact that women earn a higher percentage of baccalaureate and master's degrees and an equivalent percentage of doctoral degrees when compared to men (Lapovskey, 2009).

The term "glass ceiling" refers to the invisible barriers that obstruct women and minorities from ascending to senior leadership positions regardless of their levels of training, credentials, or achievements. Cotter, Hermsen, Ovadia, and Vanneman (2001) propose four criteria that must be present to determine that a glass ceiling exists. Criterion one proposes that a gender or racial difference exists when non-employment cannot be explained by other employee characteristics. For example, imagine two candidates apply for the same upper-level position. They are identical in every way, age, education, previous work experience, with the only difference being in either gender or race. In cases such as these, the white male will often receive an employment offer before the other applicants simply on the basis of the obscure barrier to women and minorities. The second criterion proposes that a gender or racial difference has a greater effect on obtaining more valuable outcomes (e.g., management positions) as compared to less valuable outcomes (e.g., entry-level positions). For example, fewer women hold full professor titles compared to their male counterparts (Johnson, 2016; Kena et al., 2014; Nidiffer, 2010). However, as one moves down the academic ladder white women are employed at higher rates than white males as assistant professors, instructors, and lecturers (Kena et al., 2014). Minority women are underrepresented across all ranks. Criterion three proposes that gender or race reduces the chances of promotion up the organizational ladder. For instance, women of color are the least likely to be promoted to higher ranks. When tenure track and administrative positions open up, as history shows, they will continue to go to white males unless there is a change in the way leadership is viewed. Lastly, criterion four proposes that this discrimination will progress throughout one's career. This factor is influenced by all of the previous factors. For example, women and minorities' career trajectories are flatter relative to white men.

Research also shows that there has been an inherent bias toward selecting agentic (i.e., masculine) traits for leadership (Eagly & Carli, 2007; Koenig, Eagly, Mitchell & Ristikari, 2011). Generally, men were perceived to be more assertive, decisive, and self-confident (Eagly & Carli, 2007). In contrast, women were typically ascribed communal qualities, and portrayed as kind, nurturant, sympathetic to others, and more relationship-oriented overall (Lopez & Ensari, 2014; Rosette & Tost, 2010). This bias is central to Eagly and Karau's (2002) role congruity model which proposed that the incongruence between gender roles and the perception of a successful leader results in two prejudices against women. These prejudices include that women are perceived less favorably as being able to occupy a leadership position successfully, and that they are judged less favorably when displaying the precise agentic behaviors that are perceived to be needed for a leadership role (Koenig et al., 2011).

Much of the literature has concluded that this alleged incongruence does disadvantage women when they are considered for leadership positions (Eagly & Karau, 2002; Heilman, 2001; Rosette & Tost, 2010). On the other hand, a different perspective suggests that the role congruity model can theoretically result in a leadership advantage for females (Eagly, 2007; Eagly & Carli, 2003a, 2003b; Rosette & Tost, 2010) because it posits that women are better suited to managing modern organizations because of their communal traits and willingness to adopt a transformational leadership style (Eagly, Johannesen-Schmidt, & Van Engen, 2003; Paustian-Underdahl, Walker, & Woehr, 2014). A recent meta-analysis by Paustian-Underdahl et al. (2014) examined how various contextual moderators (i.e., time of study, type of organization, hierarchical level, study setting, percent of male raters, and rating source) affected the perception of leadership skills amongst men and women. The researchers found that women were seen as more effective leaders only when "rating source" was considered as a moderating variable. However, when all moderating variables were considered, there were no significant overall gender differences. It is ironic, however, that a double standard is often applied to female leaders. Though they may be acknowledged as competent to lead effectively, women are often lambasted as being unfavorable leaders who elicit negative reactions from their subordinates (Heilman, 2001; Rosette & Tost, 2010; Vinkenburg, Van Engen, Eagly, & Johannesen-Schmidt, 2011).

Culture changes over time and, indeed, role incongruity in relation to leadership appears to have lessened for women over the past several years. Koenig et al. (2011) have outlined several theories to explain why this has occurred. First, contemporary models of effective managerial leadership have shifted to a more democratic style of leadership, one in which members of the group take a part in the decision-making process, as compared to autocratic leadership styles, which are described as more authoritarian and controlling styles that often negatively affect employee satisfaction and motivation (Koenig et al., 2011; Lopez & Ensari, 2014). Second, the mere presence of women occupying management positions may influence and lessen stereotypic beliefs about their leadership skills. Indeed, younger generations are consistently shifting to more egalitarian views of gender roles (Donnelly et al., 2016).

Women in Academic Leadership Positions

Considering the progress women have made in the field of higher education, one may posit that gender inequality issues in academia have been resolved. But, in reality, how much has changed? Do women achieve positions of leadership equal to those of men in academia? Have they obtained upper-level leadership positions in higher education? A number of women who have become college and university presidents has increased significantly from 5% in 1975 to 23% in 2006 (AACU, 2011) and then to 26.4% in 2011 (S. Cook, 2012b). However, despite this apparent increase in the attainment of prestigious, academic positions for women, their advancement still lags behind that of their male counterparts (Curtis, 2011). This point is exemplified by the fact that in 2011, the highest number of women presidents was at junior/associate colleges as opposed to universities (S. Cook, 2012b). While the percentages of women currently holding university presidency positions is not equal to those of men, their prevalence in other senior academic positions is greater (Curtis, 2011). In 2007, women constituted 38% of CAOs, 50% of central senior academic affairs officers, and 36% of academic deans (King & Gomez, 2008). Although slight increases in the number of women serving as CAOs have occurred in private and public institutions, the percentage of women holding CAO positions in doctoral degree-granting institutions decreased from 2008 to 2013 (Johnson, 2016). Additionally, the prevalence of women holding positions on college and university governing boards has stalled, with women constituting only 30% of board memberships during the past two decades (Johnson, 2016). Men still outnumber women by more than two to one in both private and public college and university governing boards (Johnson, 2016).

Pathways to Leadership

The pathways to achieve these leadership positions differ for men and women. Generally, women must establish themselves as scholars before they can reach the top academic position (S. Cook, 2012b). Achieving the rank of a full professor can extend one's opportunities for leadership in higher education, and it is also a conventional prerequisite for being promoted to a position of leadership (B. Cook, 2012a). If women strive to attain the rank of a full professor, their chances for becoming a college president can also increase. In general, women take more time than men to climb the leadership ladder. For example, women presidents are more likely to have served more time in a classroom or lab when compared to male presidents (S. Cook, 2012b). Additionally, three-fourths of women university presidents as compared to two-thirds of their male counterparts have longer experience as faculty members before becoming a university president (S. Cook, 2012b). Also, women are more likely to have spent more time serving as a provost or senior executive in academic affairs before attaining the presidency of a college/university (Johnson, 2016).

Racial Disparity

In 2011, 86.4% of college and university presidents were Caucasian, 5.9% were African American, and 3.8% were Hispanic (S. Cook, 2012b). During that year women constituted only 26.4% of college and university presidents. Of these women presidents, 38.7% were Hispanic, 34% were African American, 25.1% were Caucasian, and 20% were Asian American (S. Cook, 2012b). While these figures augur well for the presence of minority women as university presidents, unfortunately the number of racial and ethnic minority women university presidents diminished from 13.6% in 2006 to 12.6% in 2011 (S. Cook, 2012b). Additionally, Hispanic women were more likely to serve as presidents at schools granting associate degrees, while African American women are more likely to be presidents at schools granting bachelor's and master's degrees (S. Cook, 2012b). In 2013, full-time faculty in institutions of higher education consisted of 79% Caucasians (43% White males versus 35% White females), 6% African-Americans, 5% Hispanics, and 10% Asians/Pacific Islanders. Caucasians (58% male versus 26% female) comprised 84% full-time faculty members as compared to 4% African-Americans, 3% Hispanics, 9% Asians/Pacific Islanders, and less than 1% Native Americans (Kena et al., 2014). These data suggest that women and minorities are highly underrepresented amongst postsecondary academic faculty members.

Salary Disparity

There are also disparities in salary between men and women in academia. Full-time women employees were paid only 79% of what their male counterparts were paid in 2014 (American Association of University Women [AAUW], 2015). This pay gap was worst for African American, Hispanic, Native American, and Native Hawaiian women. Although the salary disparity between men and women has reduced from 41% in the 1970s to 21% in 2014, progress has stalled in recent years (AAUW, 2015). Therefore, it can be seen that women in academic professions still often experience pay inequity issues. Research has repeatedly suggested that female professors are consistently paid less than male professors (Barbezat & Hughes, 2005; Perna, 2001, Thornton, 2010). This gap in salary exists even after controlling for differences in factors such as the institutional type, faculty rank, and faculty productivity (Nettles, Perna, & Bradburn, 2000; O'Keefe & Wang, 2013). The average salary for full-time male faculty members has been higher than their female counterparts in all of the years between 1993–1994 and 2013–2014. The average salary was $85,500 for male professors and $70,400 for female professors in 2013–2014 (Kena et al., 2014). These figures suggest that pay scales have increased only 9% for female professors since the 1993–1994 academic year. Also, women with more experience at each academic rank have lower salaries than males as a result of high initial salary gaps (Perna, 2001).

Theoretical Framework Underlying Salary Disparities

What factors account for the differences in faculty salaries? In the past, researchers have proposed two theoretical approaches to explain these differences. One is human capital theory and the other is structural theory (Perna, 2001). Human capital theory suggests that an individual's employment status is dependent upon his/her personal attributes, productivity, and skills. Productivity levels are a function of an individual's efforts, educational level, on-the-job training, prior work experience, and their physical and mental health (Becker, 1962). The human capital theory has been criticized for its failure to address occupational sex segregation and lower returns to educational investments for minorities and women (DeYoung, 1989). The salary differentials between men and women are also unexplained by this theoretical approach (Umbach, 2006). On the other hand, the structural theory proposes that labor market inequalities develop due to organizational characteristics which include structuring positions and sorting employees (Youn, 1992). According to this model, differences between male and female faculty salaries occur due to the concentration of women in institutions and academic fields that have less prestige (Smart, 1991). Some theorists argue that societal pressures socialize women and minorities into academic fields and teaching positions that are less prestigious, and as a result, they earn less than male faculty members (O'Meara, Terosky, and Neumann, 2008). For example, women faculty members may not play an active role in earning the position of a full-time professor in order to maintain a balance between work and family (Ward & Wolf-Wendel, 2012). Decisions such as these can prevent women from attaining upper-level faculty positions in higher education, and due to this, their salaries may be lower than male faculty members.

Position Advancement Disparity

As previously noted, the number of doctoral degrees conferred upon women in the United States has recently become equivalent to those conferred upon men. However, the number of women who hold higher positions within academia, such as those of full professor and dean is vastly different when compared to men of similar backgrounds and qualifications. While this disparity has been known and acknowledged for quite some time, there has been little formal research exploring the actual cause(s) of this inequality. In a recent study conducted in New Zealand, 26 female professors representative of all eight of the country's universities helped to identify the possible causes of such an inequity. The study examined a multitude of work and non-work-related factors, which either helped or hindered a female's advancement at each university. Upon further analysis, five common themes emerged that contributed to their vocational positions in the hierarchy of academia. These themes included work relationships, university environment, invisible rules, proactivity, and personal circumstances (Airini et al., 2010).

In this study, "Work Relationships" consisted of collegial relationships with seniors, collegial relationships with peers, and relationships with unsupportive colleagues. Typically, collegial relationships with seniors and peers increase the advancement of women's leadership roles in universities. In contrast, the presence of unsupportive colleagues hinders this advancement. The second theme "University Environment" referred to the university-level policies and practices, as well as day-to-day application of these policies and practices. Generally, university-level policies and practices were not particularly supportive of women's advancement in leadership roles. Eight of ten incidents reported under the subcategory of policies and practices were thought to have been a hindrance for occupational advancement. These incidents included negative attitudes toward woman having children or women taking a maternity leave, negative attitudes toward women who were sick, poor systems for dealing with allegations of misbehavior, etc. On the other hand, day-to-day administration of policies and practices helps women's advancement in leadership roles. These day-to-day administrations include arrangements such as providing mentoring on how to conduct research presentations at conferences. The third theme "Invisible Rules" pertained to the reality of academia as compared with its myths. This means that while policies and procedures for promotion may exist, the interpretation of these rules may be differentially applied and there may be some "unspoken" rules. Sometimes this is referred to as "playing the game." This means that women must learn the rules about academic realities and the need to be realistic about academic gains and trade-offs. Women who understand such patterns of behavior have a higher chance of advancing to leadership positions. The fourth theme "Proactivity" was separated into four subcategories: (1) planned proactivity, (2) spontaneous proactivity, (3) professional development, and (4) change in attitude. In this context, proactivity referred to women taking responsibility for their advancement to leadership roles instead of relying on other people or situations for this advancement. The first subcategory, "planned proactivity" referred to women predetermining courses of action that help them advance to leadership roles. These actions included setting priorities, viewing oneself as a professor, making a decision to focus on research by not taking a managerial role. Generally, planned proactivity helps women progress to leadership roles. The second subcategory, "spontaneous proactivity" relates to spontaneous actions in which women recognized an opportunity and acted swiftly to capitalize on it. Such actions are helpful toward women's advancement in leadership. The third subcategory, professional development referred to women's advancement in leadership through formal and informal actions. These actions included willing to grab immediate opportunities, improving time management, and learning from mentors. Such actions help women advance their careers. The fourth subcategory, "change in attitude" can help or hinder the advancement of women in leadership roles. For example, when one realizes the significance of fostering one's development, she can advance to leadership positions. On the other hand, certain attitudes can hinder one's advancement to leadership positions. For example, attitudes such as not willing to reapply for a leadership position after rejection may hinder one's advancement to leadership roles. The last theme identified in this study was "Personal Circumstances" which included things such as personal relationships, ill health, having children, and parental leave. Circumstances such as these typically hinder the advancement of women to leadership positions. This study is important because it not only identified factors that can hinder women from advancement in the academic workplace, but also shed light on what circumstances and behaviors were helpful.

Other factors that appeared to contravene women faculty members' advancement in the leadership domains within academia have included historical inequalities, stereotypical notions about women's leadership styles, and the male dominated history of academia (Klotz 2014). Traditionally, typically, males have been thought to be independent, task oriented, and act according to reason. Females were considered more nurturant, expressive, and thought to behave more communally (Valian, 2005). While the majority of society no longer adheres to these notions, such attitudes toward females are often endorsed at leadership levels both implicitly and explicitly, particularly within the realm of academia. Let's examine the potential consequences of such notions.

Of great importance is the effect that this disparity has on academia as a whole. Although we know there are also large discrepancies between men and women in many other fields, the gender in balance in academia is of particular concern. As women continue to be underrepresented at the higher levels of academia, we develop several potential risks. First, we risk overlooking the qualities and skills possessed by such woman to advance their respective institutions. Second, we risk the possibility of losing women to sectors outside academia where they have better opportunities for advancement and financial gain. While the other sectors may gain from this inequity, it will come at great expense to the future education of our country.

Gender Differences in Achieving Tenure

In addition to less overall representation of women in higher levels of academia, there is also a great disparity between women and men with respect to the attainment of tenure. Tenure is essentially a contract that ensures a permanent position or status of employment for professors. After a probationary period of 5–7 years, a professor is eligible for such a promotion. Typically, tenure is bestowed upon those who demonstrate achievement in teaching, scholarly activity and service to the university and community at large. The National Center for Education Statistics (2000) reported that females were less likely than their male counterparts to be granted tenure (42% of females versus 66% of males). Each university has requirements for tenure that need to be met although the criteria vary from school to school. The fact that there are significantly fewer female mentors put women at a disadvantage for promotion from day 1 of their employment. After the 5- to 7-year probationary period is complete, a decision is made to either offer or decline tenure. If a negative decision is made, it is common for a 1-year terminal appointment to be bestowed upon the professor. This year gives a professor the opportunity to explore other career options and seek professorship at another university.

Some universities have started to extend the "tenure clock" for a number of reasons. Adding additional time to this "tenure clock" allows more flexibility for those professors who may need to put the advancement of their careers on hold for a certain amount of time. Such issues may range from things such as sick leave due to significant illness, family leave, and childrearing leave. The latter, for the purpose of this chapter is of greatest importance. The attainment of tenure is difficult enough to achieve, but when one factors in the initial year that is optimally needed to support a child's development, it is not surprising that men outnumber women as tenured professors. At The University of Michigan, if not recommended for tenure in the sixth or seventh year of their probationary period, faculty members are being offered a time extension not to exceed a total of 10 years. Another alternative is being offered wherein a faculty member is given the choice of a 1-year terminal appointment, so long as it is served within the University's 10-year tenure track (Weiss, Haskell, Pierce, & Whitman, 2012). Some universities refer to this extension as "stopping the clock." Theoretically, stopping the clock due to personal decisions or familial responsibilities should not prejudice one's promotion or tenure. However, even if taking only childrearing into account, stopping the clock appears to impact females more negatively than males.

Also noteworthy is the disparity of the number of women of color employed in American colleges and universities. At the turn of the century, 72% of tenured full professors were White men, 17% were White women, 8% consisted of African American, Hispanic, and Native American men, and only 2% of tenured full professors were females of non-Caucasian ethnicities (Evans, 2007). It has been nearly 100 years since women earned the right to vote, and over 60 years since the de-segregation of our schools. Why then, has it taken so long for our country to achieve equality with respect to our university educators? Evans (2007) has suggested that gender and cultural diversity in higher education is essential to the intellectual health of every campus. As institutions responsible for the growth and development of our country, colleges and universities should be at the forefront of advancing of education, rather than hindering it.

Family Structures

Gender roles can be defined as the particular traits, mannerisms, interests, attitudes, and behaviors which are considered by one's culture to be either "male" or "female." (Wienclaw, 2015). As stated previously, these traditional norms assign gender roles described as agentic for men and communal for women (Koenig et al., 2011). Accordingly, in traditional western cultures, men have historically been expected to be the breadwinners, whereas women were expected to be the primary caretakers of the household and the children. However, major changes occurred with respect to gender role expectations during the mid-1960s. More women were employed outside the home in order to earn financial resources for their families (Moen, Erickson, & Dempster-McClain, 1997). Over the past decades, a major shift to dual-career families has evolved. Additionally, the number of single-parent households has increased. Due to these transformations, family responsibilities often are not evenly shared. Instead, women are expected to be the homemakers and the bread-winners of the family (Dempsey, 2002).

Family Patterns of Women with Leadership Positions in Academia

Women's attainment of the position of University President has proceeded slowly during the past four decades. The Higher Education Resource Services (HERS) sought to find reasons why women's progression into the university presidency positions has been difficult (White, 2013). They interviewed 35 women university leaders of different ages, institutional backgrounds, and ethnicities to learn about factors that assisted or disrupted their advancement to top-level leadership positions in academia. In addition, two hundred women at various stages of their career were interviewed who were potential candidates for leadership positions. The data suggested that senior women leaders (presidents, chancellors, provosts, and vice presidents) were highly motivated to learn, change, and serve. Moreover, these women viewed higher education as a tool to transform the lives of individuals living in communities where opportunities were unevenly divided (White, 2013). Also, they were exceptional role models because they developed pronounced political skills that helped them prosper in challenging leadership environments. However, in spite of the existence of such role models, younger women are still faced with finding methods that can aid them in maintaining a balance between their professional and family lives (White, 2013).

Women in academia are often faced with the dilemma of sacrificing traditional family life in order to achieve leadership positions. As noted above, many women want to maintain a balance between their professional and family lives. However, such a balance is often difficult to maintain if they desire to advance to top-level leadership positions in institutions of higher education. Judith White, the president and executive director of HERS believes that the "we can do it all" and "have it all" myth is a dangerous one (White, 2013). Data that support this caveat include the facts that women university presidents and CAOs are less likely to be married or have children than their male counterparts (Johnson, 2016). In general, women in academia between the ages of 35 and 50 reported having fewer children than women physicians, lawyers, doctors, and chief executives of the same ages (Mason & Goulden, 2004). Additionally, women in academia at top-level positions are more likely to have adjusted their careers based upon their family needs (Johnson, 2016).

A large number of women who may possess incredible leadership skills are unable to advance to upper-level positions in their academic career. This may occur as a result of the choices they need to make for their families. These decisions include not playing an active role for promotion to full-time professorship in order to maintain an equilibrium between work and home or giving up full-time positions due to lack of childcare options (Ward & Wolf-Wendel, 2012). Women faculty members, as compared to male faculty members, may be differentially affected by conflicts that arise from family and work obligations (American Association of University Professors [AAUP], 2001). They are often responsible for more household responsibilities than their husbands. For example, women scientists working at high-level US research institutions do double the household chores when compared to their husbands, who are also scientists (Schiebinger & Gilmartin, 2010). Events such as pregnancy, childbirth, and child rearing create even greater interruptions in the progressions of the careers of women professors. These events can restrict the ability of women to enter careers such as science and engineering that often require frequent travel (Caprile & Vallés, 2010).

Federal and State Laws for Family Care and Disability Services

A variety of federal and state policies exist that can assist women in obtaining paid and unpaid leaves for family leave, but these policies provide minimum benefits (AAUP, 2001). Some of these laws include the Pregnancy Discrimination Act (PDA) and the Family and Medical Leave Act (FMLA). The Pregnancy Discrimination Act (1978) forbids discrimination against pregnant women. This act is an amendment to the Title VII of the Civil Rights Act of 1964 which prohibits sex discrimination on the basis of pregnancy, childbirth, or related medical conditions. Based on this act, pregnancy and childbirth are considered to be types of physical disabilities. Hence, pregnant women professors should be permitted to receive paid disability leave (AAUP, 2001).

The FMLA (1993) authorizes eligible male and female employees to take an unpaid leave, or to substitute applicable accrued paid leave, for a total of 12 work weeks in a single 12-month period to care for newborns or newly adopted infants, to care for the employee's parent, spouse, son, or daughter with a serious health condition, when the employee is incapable of working due to his/her own serious health condition, or for demanding situations arising out of the fact that the employee's, parent, spouse, son, daughter, is an active military member. The FMLA also allows eligible employees to take up to 26 work weeks of FMLA leave in a 12-month period in order to care for their parent, spouse, son, or daughter if they are covered military members with a serious illness or injury. Before March 2015, the FMLA did not apply to same-sex legally married couples. On February 25, 2015, the Department of Labor issued a Final Rule that revised the definition of spouse under the FMLA of 1993. This Final Rule was made effective on March 27, 2015 which allows for eligible employees in legal same-sex marriages to fully practice their FMLA rights.

In addition to federal and state laws for family care and disability acts, the AAUP encourages institutions of higher education to adopt other family-friendly policies that can offer greater support for academic professionals and faculty members (AAUP, 2001). Some universities that have followed this approach include the

University of Michigan, Washington and Lee University, and Princeton University. At the University of Michigan, faculty members can use the school's "Family Helpers" database to obtain a list of students who are ready to assist them with babysitting, cleaning the house, or other household responsibilities (Novotney, 2010). At Washington and Lee University of Virginia, faculty members are permitted to make the use of conference calls and Internet chats with their students if a family emergency occurs (Novotney, 2010). Finally, at Princeton University, faculty/staff members and students are given opportunities to receive free flu shots (Novotney, 2010). Although such programs exist, some universities and colleges do not have significant family-friendly policies for working families. A survey conducted by the Center for the Education of Women at the University of Michigan suggested that the average university offers only 1.9 out of 7 potential family-friendly policies (University of Michigan, 2007). Hence, women working in such institutions may lack the support that could assist them in their goal to become full-time professors and to advance to leadership positions within academia.

Academic Field Disparity

As of 2012 26% of university presidents were women (S. Cook, 2012b). However, that number had increased only three percentage points since 2006 (S. Cook, 2012b). Looking at these statistics, one may ask why so few women have advanced to the highest position of leadership in academia. The increase of the advancement of women is low, but even more disconcerting is the number of women leaders located in prestigious institutions. In 2011, a third of associate/community colleges were led by women. Moreover, women compose half of the CAOs at community colleges (Eckel, Cook, & King, 2009). In contrast, the number of women presidents at 4-year public institutions actually dropped significantly from 34% in 2006 to 28% in 2011 (S. Cook, 2012b). Also, women compose only one-third of CAOs at 4-year universities (Eckel et al., 2009). This suggests that women are not making progress breaking the glass ceiling to enter the position of university president, and as a result, are highly underrepresented in the leadership positions at top-academic institutions. Additionally, the percentage of women of color (African-Americans, Hispanics, Asian Americans, or American Indians) hired in those leadership positions also appears to be decreasing (S. Cook, 2012b).

Although a high number of women are represented in postsecondary degree-granting institutions, they are underrepresented in the science, technology, engineering, and mathematics (STEM) fields. If we closely look at these disciplines, it is clear that the number of women in these fields is low. While women earned more than half of the bachelor's degrees awarded in the biological sciences, only 18.2% of them received degrees in computer sciences, 19.2% in engineering, 19.1% in physics, and 43.1% in mathematics and other sciences (National Center for Science and Engineering Statistics [NCSES], 2015). Although women are underrepresented in the disciplines just mentioned, they are overrepresented in the social sciences and the biosciences (excluding economics). Women account for approximately 70% of psychology graduates at each degree level (NCSES, 2015). A similar pattern of the underrepresentation of women is also observed in the STEM workforce. Although the number of women working in the science and engineering workforce has increased during the past years, gender disparities continue to exist in the engineering, computer science, and the physical science departments of academia (National Science Board, 2014). While women are more likely to be employed in a health-related profession, they are less likely than men to work as physicians, surgeons, or dentists (NCSES, 2015).

The past two decades have witnessed a growth of women's participation in the academic doctoral workforce. Despite this progress, women and minorities (Blacks, Hispanics, Native Americans, Alaskan Natives, Native Hawaiians, and Other Pacific Islanders) are underrepresented in academic employment when compared to their male, White, and Asian counterparts (NCSES, 2015). These disparities are prominent in areas such as rank, income, and federal support. Women are also less likely to hold full professorship positions in the country's most intensive research academic institutions (NCSES, 2015), and thus are more likely to be employed as full-time associate and assistant professors. This pattern occurs, in part, because older cohorts of faculty members in engineering, science, and healthcare are nearly exclusively male (NCSES, 2015).

When considering these data, one might wonder when women will be equally represented in STEM disciplines. Increasing the number of women in STEM fields is imperative since it will be beneficial in a number of ways. For example, the diversity and supportive environments for students will improve with the addition of more women and minorities in STEM disciplines in higher education. These women and minorities will prove to be effective role models and mentors to students who are members of underrepresented groups. Programs such as ADVANCE created by the National Science Foundation can help increase the number of women, minority women, and women with disabilities in STEM faculty and leadership positions. This is a federally funded program which was created in 2001 in order to implement various strategies that can affect leadership development and work-life balance for the groups mentioned above. More than 100 higher education institutions are participants of this program, and it has optimistically impacted an exceptional number of women and men. For example, it has expanded the representation of women and women minorities in the STEM careers. This increase has helped diversify the science and engineering workforce. It has also increased the participation of women in the STEM disciplines due to which the status of women faculty in these fields has advanced. Also, this program has encouraged and continues to encourage higher education institutions to address various issues such as childbearing that affect STEM women faculty.

Conclusions

Gender disparity amongst leadership positions differ in many sectors. However, they are particularly alarming amongst university educators and higher level positions within the realm of Academia such as Dean, Provost, or President. With females now outnumbering males in college attendance and graduation rates, one would expect that an increased number of women faculty members and academic leaders would also exist in this nation's postsecondary education system. While the number of doctoral degrees conferred upon men and women is nearly equal in America, the gender representation in Academia remains skewed where men still comprise the majority of full professors, deans, and university presidents.

Significant differences in salary between men and women are also present at nearly every academic standing above assistant professor. There is a salary gap of over 20% for women in academia as compared to men, and although this is much smaller than in the past, it has not been rectified within universities. Not surprisingly, this gap is even greater amongst academic women of color. Females are consistently being paid less than their male counterparts, in spite of equal experience and competency. And because females often begin their careers being paid less than their male counterparts, they continue to be paid less as female associate or full professors than males of the same rank. There are also disparities between the number of women and men awarded tenure, with 20% fewer women being tenured despite qualifications equivalent to those of males. Some of this may be due to the fact that there are fewer female mentors within universities, and therefore fewer higher level faculty members to facilitate the advancement of their junior women faculty members. It is past time for women to be represented in this country's institutions of higher learning in accord with their skills and their representation in the general population. While many factors have contributed to this inequality, it still appears that that many of our society's ideals of traditional gender roles continue to prevent women from attaining the status they deserve. Clearly, in this the twenty-first century, it is time for Academia to rectify the differential treatment of women in academia so that egalitarian leadership can be accomplished.

References

Airini, Collings, S., Conner, L., McPherson, K., Midson, B., & Wilson, C. (2010). Learning to be leaders in higher education: What helps or hinders women's advancement as leaders in universities. *Educational Management Administration & Leadership, 39*(1), 44–62. https://doi.org/10.1177/1741143210383896.

Association of American College and Universities. (2011). Forty years of change: Highlights from the data. *On Campus with Women, 39*(3). Retrieved from http://archive.aacu.org/ocww/volume39_3/data.cfm.

American Association of University Professors (AAUP). (2001). Statement of principles on family responsibilities and academic work. *Academe, 87*(5), 55–61. Retrieved from http://www.jstor.org/stable/i40009828.

American Association of University Women. (2015). *The simple truth about the gender pay gap.* Retrieved from http://www.aauw.org/resource/the-simple-truth-about-the-gender-pay-gap/.

Barbezat, D. A., & Hughes, J. W. (2005). Salary structure effects and the gender pay gap in academia. *Research in Higher Education, 46*(6), 621–640. https://doi.org/10.1007/s11162-004-4137-1.

Becker, G. S. (1962). Investment in human capital: A theoretical analysis. *Journal of Political Economy, 70*(5, Part 2), 9–49.

Caprile, M., & Vallés, N. (2010). *Science as a labour activity. Meta-analysis of gender and science research—Topic report*. Luxembourg: Publications Office of the European Union. Retrieved from http://meta-analysisofgenderandscienceresearch.org/doc/TR4_Labour.pdf.

Chin, J. L. (2011). Women and leadership: Transforming visions and current contexts. *Forum on Public Policy Online, 2011*(2), 1–12.

Cook, B. J. (2012a). The American college president study: Key findings and takeaways. *The Presidency, 15*(Suppl. 2). Retrieved from http://www.acenet.edu/the-presidency/Pages/Spring-Supplement-2012.aspx.

Cook, S. G. (2012b). Women presidents: Now 26.4% but still underrepresented. *Women in Higher Education, 21*(5), 1–3. https://doi.org/10.1002/whe.10322.

Cotter, D. A., Hermsen, J. M., Ovadia, S., & Vanneman, R. (2001). The glass ceiling effect. *Social Forces, 80*(2), 655–681. https://doi.org/10.1353/sof.2001.0091.

Curtis, J. W. (2011, April). Persistent inequity: Gender and academic employment. *New Voices in Pay Equity*. Symposium conducted at the meeting of American Association of University Women, Washington, DC.

Dempsey, K. (2002). Who gets the best deal from marriage: Women or men? *Journal of Sociology, 38*(2), 91–110. https://doi.org/10.1177/144078302128756525.

DeYoung, A. J. (1989). *Economics and American education: A historical and critical overview of the impact of economic theories on schooling in the United States*. United Kingdom: Longman Publishing Group.

Donnelly, K., Twenge, J. M., Clark, M. A., Shaikh, S. K., Beiler-May, A., & Carter, N. T. (2016). Attitudes toward women's work and family roles in the United States, 1976–2013. *Psychology of Women Quarterly, 40*(1), 41–54. https://doi.org/10.1177/0361684315590774.

Eagly, A. H. (2007). Female leadership advantage and disadvantage: Resolving the contradictions. *Psychology of Women Quarterly, 31*, 1–12. https://doi.org/10.1111/j.1471-6402.2007.00326.x.

Eagly, A. H., & Carli, L. L. (2003a). The female leadership advantage: An evaluation of the evidence. *The Leadership Quarterly, 14*, 807–834. https://doi.org/10.1016/j.leaqua.2003.09.004.

Eagly, A. H., & Carli, L. L. (2003b). Finding gender advantage and disadvantage: Systematic research integration is the solution. *The Leadership Quarterly, 14*, 851–859. https://doi.org/10.1016/j.leaqua.2003.09.003.

Eagly, A. H., & Carli, L. L. (2007). Women and the labyrinth of leadership. *Harvard Business Review, 85*(9), 63–71. https://doi.org/10.1108/hrmid.2008.04416aad.004.

Eagly, A. H., & Karau, S. J. (2002). Role congruity theory of prejudice toward female leaders. *Psychological Review, 109*(3), 573–598. https://doi.org/10.1037/0033-295x.109.3.573.

Eagly, A. H., Johannesen-Schmidt, M. C., & Van Engen, M. L. (2003). Transformational, transactional, and laissez-faire leadership styles: A meta-analysis comparing women and men. *Psychological Bulletin, 129*(4), 569–591. https://doi.org/10.1037/0033-2909.129.4.569.

Eckel, P. D., Cook, B. J., & King, J. E. (2009). *The CAO census: A national profile of chief academic officers*. Washington, DC: American Council on Education.

Evans, S. Y. (2007). Women of color in American higher education. *Thought & Action, 23*, 131–138. Retrieved from https://www.nea.org/home/33193.htm.

Heilman, M. E. (2001). Description and prescription: How gender stereotypes prevent women's ascent up the organizational ladder. *Journal of Social Issues, 57*(4), 657–674. https://doi.org/10.1111/0022-4537.00234.

Hesse-Biber, S. (2012). Feminist approaches to triangulation: Uncovering subjugated knowledge and fostering social change in mixed methods research *Journal of Mixed Methods Research, 6*(2), 137–146.

Johnson, H. L. (2016). *Pipelines, pathways, and institutional leadership: An update on the status of women in higher education*. Washington, DC: American Council on Education. Retrieved from http://www.acenet.edu/news-room/Documents/Higher-Ed-Spotlight-Pipelines-Pathways-and-Institutional-Leadership-Status-of-Women.pdf.

Kena, G., Aud, S., Johnson, F., Wang, X., Zhang, J., Rathbun, A., & Kristapovich, P. (2014). *The condition of education 2014 (NCES 2014–083)*. Retrieved from National Center for Education Statistics website: http://nces.ed.gov/pubsearch.

King, J. E., & Gomez, G. G. (2008). *On the pathway to the presidency: Characteristics of higher education's senior leadership*. Washington, DC: American Council on Education. Retrieved from https://www.cupahr.org/knowledgecenter/files/PathwayPresidency.pdf.

Klotz, A. M. (2014). *The journey to the top: Women's paths to the university presidency*. Doctoral dissertation. Available from ProQuest Dissertations & Theses Global. (1535703889) (Accession or Order No.).

Koenig, A. M., Eagly, A. H., Mitchell, A. A., & Ristikari, T. (2011). Are leader stereotypes masculine? A meta-analysis of three research paradigms. *Psychological Bulletin, 137*(4), 616–642. https://doi.org/10.1037/a0023557.

Lapovskey, L. (2009). *The White House project report: Benchmarking women's leadership*. Washington, DC: Council of Economic Advisers. Retrieved from https://www.whitehouse.gov/administration/eop/cea/factsheets-reports.

Lopez, E. S., & Ensari, N. (2014). The effects of leadership style, organizational outcome, and gender on attributional bias toward leaders. *Journal of Leadership Studies, 8*(2), 19–37. https://doi.org/10.1002/jls.21326.

Mason, M. A., & Goulden, M. (2004). Marriage and baby blues: Redefining gender equity in the academy. *The Annals of the American Academy of Political and Social Science, 596*(1), 86–103. https://doi.org/10.1177/0002716204268744.

Moen, P., Erickson, M. A., & Dempster-Mcclain, D. (1997). Their mother's daughters? The intergenerational transmission of gender attitudes in a world of changing roles. *Journal of Marriage and the Family, 59*(2), 281–293. https://doi.org/10.2307/353470.

Morley, L. (2006). Hidden transcripts: The micro-politics of gender in commonwealth universities. *Women's Studies International Forum, 29*(6), 543–551. https://doi.org/10.1016/j.wsif.2006.10.007.

National Center for Science and Engineering Statistics. (2015). *Women, minorities, and persons with disabilities in science and engineering: 2015 (NSF Report No.15–311)*. Arlington, VA: National Science Foundation. Retrieved from http://www.nsf.gov/statistics/2015/nsf15311/.

National Science Board. (2014). *Science and engineering indicators 2014 (NSB 14–01)*. Arlington, VA: National Science Foundation. Retrieved from http://www.nsf.gov/statistics/seind14/index.cfm/home.

National Science Foundation. (2008). *ADVANCE: Increasing the participation and advancement of women in academic science and engineering careers* (NSF publication 07–582). Retrieved from http://www.nsf.gov/pubs/2007/nsf07582/nsf07582.pdf.

Nettles, M. T., Perna, L. W., & Bradburn, E. M. (2000). *Salary, promotion, and tenure status of minority and women faculty in U.S. colleges and universities (NCES 2000–173)*. Washington, DC: U.S. Department of Education, Office of Educational Research and Improvement.

Nidiffer, J. (2010). Overview: Women as leaders in academia. *Gender and Women's Leadership: A Reference Handbook, 2*, 555–564. https://doi.org/10.4135/9781412979344.n58.

Novotney, A. (2010). A more family-friendly ivory tower? *Monitor on Psychology, 41*(1), 54. https://doi.org/10.1037/e640612009-027.

O'Keefe, S., & Wang, T. (2013). Publishing pays: Economists' salaries reflect productivity. *The Social Science Journal, 50*(1), 45–54. https://doi.org/10.1016/j.soscij.2012.09.008.

O'Meara, K., Terosky, A. L., & Neumann, A. (2008). Faculty careers and work lives: A professional growth perspective. *ASHE Higher Education Report, 34*(3), 1–221. https://doi.org/10.1002/aehe.3403.

Paustian-Underdahl, S. C., Walker, L. S., & Woehr, D. J. (2014). Gender and perceptions of leadership effectiveness: A meta-analysis of contextual moderators. *Journal of Applied Psychology, 99*(6), 1129–1145. https://doi.org/10.1037/a0036751.

Perna, L. W. (2001). Sex differences in faculty salaries: A cohort analysis. *The Review of Higher Education, 24*(3), 283–307. https://doi.org/10.1353/rhe.2001.0006.

Pregnancy Discrimination Act. (1978). *Pregnancy Discrimination Act of 1978, 2 U.S.C. § et seq. 2000*. Retrieved from https://www.eeoc.gov/laws/statutes/pregnancy.cfm.

Rosette, A. S., & Tost, L. P. (2010). Agentic women and communal leadership: How role prescriptions confer advantage to top women leaders. *Journal of Applied Psychology, 95*(2), 221–235. https://doi.org/10.1037/a0018204.

Schiebinger, L., & Gilmartin, S. (2010). Housework is an academic issue. *Academe, 96*(1), 39–44. Retrieved from http://www.jstor.org/stable/2069461.

Smart, J. C. (1991). Gender equity in academic rank and salary. *Review of Higher Education, 14*(4), 511–526.

Snyder, T. D., & Dillow, S. A. (2015). *Digest of Education Statistics 2013 (NCES 2014–015).* Washington, DC: National Center Education for Education Statistics. Retrieved from http://nces.ed.gov/pubsearch.

FMLA. (1993). *The Family and Medical Leave Act of 1993, 29 U.S.C. 2601 § et seq.* Retrieved from http://webapps.dol.gov/FederalRegister/PdfDisplay.aspx?DocId=28079.

Thornton, S. (2010). No refuge: The annual report on the economic status of the profession, 2009–10. *Academe, 96*(2), 4–32. Retrieved from http://www.aaup.org/sites/default/files/files/zreport_1.pdf.

Umbach, P. D. (2006). Gender equity in the academic labor market: An analysis of academic disciplines. *Research in Higher Education, 48*(2), 169–192. https://doi.org/10.1007/s11162-006-9043-2.

University of Michigan Center for the Education of Women. (2007) *Family-friendly policies in higher education: A five-year report.* Retrieved from http://cew.umich.edu/research/pubs/hepubs/climate.

U.S. Department of Education, National Center for Education Statistics. (2000). *Salary, promotion, and tenure status of minority and women faculty in U.S. colleges and universities* (NCES Publication No. 2000173). Retrieved from https://nces.ed.gov/pubsearch/pubsinfo.asp?pubid=2000173.

Valian, V. (2005). Beyond gender schemas: Improving the advancement of women in academia. *Hypatia, 20*(3), 198–213. https://doi.org/10.1111/j.1527-2001.2005.tb00495.x.

Vinkenburg, C., Van Engen, M., Eagly, A., & Johannesen-Schmidt, M. (2011). An exploration of stereotypical beliefs about leadership styles: Is transformational leadership a route to women's promotion? *The Leadership Quarterly, 22*(1), 10–21. https://doi.org/10.1016/j.leaqua.2010.12.003.

Ward, K., & Wolf-Wendel, L. (2012). *Academic motherhood: How faculty manage work and family.* New Brunswick, NJ: Rutgers University Press.

Weiss, J. A., Haskell, G., Pierce, L., & Whitman, C. (2012) *Guidelines regarding university of Michigan policies that govern time to tenure review and related matters.* Retrieved from https://www.provost.umich.edu/faculty/tenure_review/policies.html.

Wienclaw, R. A. (2015). *Gender roles.* Research Starters: Sociology (Online Edition). Ipswich, MA: EBSCO.

White, J. (2013). HERS at forty: Shaping a new vision of women's (and men's) liberation. *On Campus with Women, 41*(2–3). Retrieved from http://archive.aacu.org/ocww/archive.cfm.

Youn, T. I. (1992). The sociology of academic careers and academic labor markets. *Research in Labor Economics, 13*(1011030), 487.

Leadership Means Using the Courts to Demand Equal Enforcement of and Protection for Women's Constitutional and Civil Rights

Wendy Murphy

To handle yourself, use your head; to handle others, use your heart.

Eleanor Roosevelt

The Title IX Statute

Title IX was enacted in 1972 as an educational federal civil rights law and states that "no person shall, on the basis of sex be … subjected to discrimination." 20 U.S.C. § 1681(a); 34 C.F.R. part 106.31(a). Discrimination on the basis of sex occurs in many forms, such as sex-/gender-motivated harassment and violence, including sexual assault, and is defined as "unwelcome and offensive" words or conduct of a sexual or gender-based nature that was not requested or invited, and which an individual considered to be "undesirable or offensive." http://www2.ed.gov/about/offices/list/ocr/docs/ocrshpam.html. Title IX covers student on student sexual assaults. *Davis v. Monroe*, 526 U.S. 629 (1999).

Title IX is coextensive with Title VI[1] and Title IV of the Civil Rights Act of 1964.[2] Title IV explicitly and equally prohibits discrimination on the basis of sex, race,

[1] 34 C.F.R. § 106.71 states that the procedural provisions applicable to Title VI of the Civil Rights Act (34 CFR §§ 100.6-100.11) are adopted and incorporated therein.

[2] *See Title IX Legal Manual*, The United States Department of Justice (last visited Jan 30, 2014), http://www.justice.gov/crt/about/cor/coord/ixlegal.php (noting that "Congress consciously modeled Title IX on Title VI" and citing *Alexander v. Choate*, 469 U.S. 287, 294 (1985) (for the proposition that because Title IX and Title VI contain parallel language, the same analytic framework should apply in the context of administrative redress proceedings because both statutes were enacted to prevent unlawful discrimination and to provide remedies for the effects of past discrimination); U.S. Department of Justice, findings letter against the University of New Mexico, (April 22, 2016) (noting that Title IX, Title VI, and Title IV are coextensive civil rights laws);

W. Murphy (✉)
New England Law Boston, Boston, MA, USA
e-mail: wmurphy@nesl.edu

F. L. Denmark, M. A. Paludi (eds.), *Women and Leadership*,
https://doi.org/10.1007/978-3-319-72182-8_7

and national origin in public schools.[3] Title IX prohibits sex-based discrimination in public and private schools that receive federal funds.[4]

Long misunderstood to be primarily a sports equity rule for female athletes, Title IX was modeled after Title VI of the Civil Rights Act of 1964, which provides that "No person in the United States shall, on the ground of race, color, or national origin, be excluded from participation in, be denied the benefits of, or be subjected to discrimination under any program or activity receiving Federal financial assistance," 42 U.S.C. §§ 2000d–2000d-7, Title IX uses exactly the same enabling language and states that "No person in the United States shall, on the basis of sex, be excluded from participation in, be denied the benefits of, or be subjected to discrimination under any education program or activity receiving Federal financial assistance…" 20 U.S.C. § 1681(a).

Facts Related to the Class of Individuals Affected by the DeVos Rules

One in three to one in five women is victimized by sexual assault during college.[5] Even using the more conservative one in five number, and considering that about six million women currently are enrolled as undergraduates in 4-year schools; this

---

https://www.justice.gov/opa/file/843901/download; *Justice Department Announces Investigations of the Handling of Sexual Assault Allegations by the University of Montana, the Missoula, Mont., Police Department and the Missoula County Attorney's Office*, Department of Justice (May 1, 2012), http://www.justice.gov/opa/pr/2012/ May/12-crt-561.html (announcing Title IX compliance review and Title IV investigation of the University of Montana and noting, "Title IX of the Education Amendments of 1972 and Title IV of the Civil Rights Act of 1964 each prohibit sex discrimination, including sexual assault and sexual harassment in education programs"); *Resolution Agreement*, http://www.justice.gov/crt/about/edu/documents/ montanaagree.pdf (announcing resolution agreement with the University of Montana and noting that Title IV and Title IX are subject to the same regulations to ensure enforcement of rights regarding discrimination, harassment, and violence in education "on the basis of sex." 28 C.F.R. Part 54 and 34 C.F.R. Part 106). *See also* the Civil Rights Restoration Act of 1987, which made clear that substantive standards from Title VI apply with equal force to Title IX, 20 U.S.C. § 1687; 29 U.S.C. § 794, 42 U.S.C. § 2000d-4a, and 42 U.S.C. § 6101.

[3] Title IV prohibits discrimination in identified public entities, including schools and other "federally assisted programs," on the basis of *"race, color, sex, religion or national origin."* 42 U.S.C. §§ 2000c through 2000c-9; Equal Educational Opportunities Act of 1974, Title II, 20 U.S.C. §§ 1701–1758.

[4] 20 U.S.C., § 1681.

[5] https://www.ncjrs.gov/pdffiles1/nij/grants/221153.pdf, p. xii-xiii and 2-1 (2007); U.S. Department of Justice Office of Community Oriented Policing Services, Acquaintance Rape of College Students, March 28, 2002, http://www.cops.usdoj.gov/pdf/e03021472.pdf; https://www.ncjrs.gov/pdffiles1/nij/grants/221153.pdf; Freyd, J., Rosenthal, M., & Smith, C. (2014). *Preliminary results*

means that *more than a million of these women will experience sexual assault during college over the next 4 years*; a number substantially greater than the number of students who will suffer any other type of civil rights violence on campus. Indeed, although no formal comparative data exists, violence against women is clearly more prevalent than all other forms of civil rights harassment and violence against students from other protected class categories combined (U.S. Department of Justice 2001; report did not measure gender-based bias crimes and found an average of only 3.8 hate crimes on campus for all of 1998, for a total of 334 incidents in 411 schools. During the same time period, the FBI ascertained that 241 incidents of hate crimes were reported from 222 of 450 schools). This disturbing data has been ignored for decades even though congresswoman Shirley Chisholm remarked during congressional hearings in the early 1970s to support the passage of Title IX that she had endured far more discrimination on the basis of sex in her political career than she ever endured on the basis of her status as an African-American.[6]

By comparison, about 26,000 sexual assaults occur in the military each year,[7] which number includes not only rape and attempted rape but also relatively minor sexual touching not rising to the level of attempted rape.[8] Approximately 30% of sexual assault victims in the general population file reports.[9] A similar number of military victims file reports.[10] The number is much lower for college victims where only 5–12% of victims file reports.[11]

Female students in the United States have endured pervasive unequal treatment, harassment, and violence, on the basis of sex, throughout all levels of education.[12] Women, including female postsecondary students, suffer disproportionately high

---

from the University of Oregon sexual violence and institutional behavior campus survey. http://dynamic.uoregon.edu/jjf/campus/UO-campus- results-30Sept14.pdf; Freyd, J, et al., (2014). (one in three); Humphrey, J. A., & White J. W. (2000). (one in four); Krebs, C. P. et al. (2009). (one in five).

[6] *What former presidential candidate Shirley Chisholm said about facing gender discrimination*, September 13, 2016, PBS.org, https://www.pbs.org/newshour/politics/what-former-presidential-candidate-shirley-chisholm-said-about-facing-gender-discrimination.

[7] An estimated 26,000 sexual assaults occurred in all branches of the military in 2012, http://www.sapr.mil/public/docs/reports/FY12_DoD_SAPRO_Annual_Report_on_Sexual_Assault-VOLUME_ONE.pdf.

[8] Id.

[9] http://www.rainn.org/get-information/statistics/reporting-rates.

[10] http://www.usccr.gov/pubs/09242013_Statutory_Enforcement_Report_Sexual_Assault_ in_the_Military.pdf, p. 8.

[11] http://www.nij.gov/publications/pages/publication-detail.aspx?ncjnumber=182369 (2001) (5%); https://www.ncjrs.gov/pdffiles1/nij/grants/221153.pdf, 5–22 (2007) (12.9%).

[12] Sadker, & Zittleman. (2009). *Still Failing at Fairness, How Gender Bias Cheats Girls and Boys in School and What We Can Do About It*, Scribner Press; www.hks.harvard.edu/centers/carr/research-publications/carr-center-working-papers-series/caplan-and-ford-%22the-voices-of-diversity-%22.

rates of domestic and dating violence,[13] sexual assault,[14] and stalking.[15] In fact, according to some studies, a student is more likely to be victimized by sexual assault if she attends college than if she does not.[16]

The DeVos Rules

The DeVos rules by their terms were limited in application to sex-based harms, including "dating violence,[17] domestic violence,[18] sexual assault,[19] and stalking."[20] (DeVos rules, p.1, 2). They were issued as a seven-page document entitled "Q and

[13] Women are less likely than men to be victims of violent crimes overall, but women are 5–8 times more likely than men to be victimized by an intimate partner. *Violence by Intimates: Analysis of Data on Crimes by Current or Former Spouses, Boyfriends, and Girlfriends*, U.S. Department of Justice, March, 1998; violence by an intimate partner accounts for about 21% of violent crime experienced by women and about 2% of the violence experienced by men. *Id.* 92% of all domestic violence incidents are committed by men against women. *Violence Against Women, Bureau of Justice Statistics*, U.S. Department of Justice, January, 1994; 84% of raped women know their assailants and 57% of rapes occur on a date. Koss, M. P. (1988). Hidden rape: Incidence, prevalence and descriptive characteristics of sexual aggression and victimization in a national sample of college students. In A. W. Burgess (Ed.) *Sexual assault* (Vol. II). New York: Garland Pub.

[14] Nine out of ten rape victims are female, U.S. Department of Justice. (2003). *2003 National Crime Victimization Survey*; Women aged 16–24 are four times more likely to be raped than any other population group. Koss, M. P., *id.*

[15] 8% of women and 2% of men in the United States have been stalked at some time in their life. 78% of stalking victims identified in a survey were women, and 22% were men. Thus, four out of five stalking victims are women. By comparison, 94% of the stalkers identified by female victims and 60% of the stalkers identified by male victims were male. Overall, 87% of the stalkers identified by the victims were male. National Institute of Justice 1998. *Stalking in America: Findings from the National Violence Against Women Survey.*

[16] One in four students in the United States is victimized by rape or attempted rape during college, *see* n.1, while one in six American women is the victim of an attempted or completed rape in her lifetime. National Institute of Justice & Centers for Disease Control & Prevention. (1998). *Prevalence, Incidence and Consequences of Violence Against Women Survey.*

[17] Women are less likely than men to be victims of violent crimes overall, but women are 5–8 times more likely than men to be victimized by an intimate partner. *Violence by Intimates: Analysis of Data on Crimes by Current or Former Spouses, Boyfriends, and Girlfriends*, U.S. Department of Justice, March, 1998; violence by an intimate partner accounts for about 21% of violent crime experienced by women and about 2% of the violence experienced by men. *Id.*

[18] 92% of all domestic violence incidents are committed by men against women. *Violence Against Women, Bureau of Justice Statistics*, U.S. Department of Justice, January, 1994; 84% of raped women know their assailants and 57% of rapes occur on a date. Koss, M. P. (1988). Hidden rape: Incidence, prevalence and descriptive characteristics of sexual aggression and victimization in a national sample of college students. In A. W. Burgess (ed.) *Sexual assault* (Vol. II). New York: Garland Pub.

[19] Nine out of ten rape victims are female, U.S. Department of Justice. (2003). *2003 National Crime Victimization Survey*; Women aged 16–24 are four times more likely to be raped than any other population group. Koss, M. P., *id.*

[20] 8% of women and 2% of men in the United States have been stalked at some time in their life. 78% of stalking victims identified in a survey were women, and 22% were men. Thus, four out of

A on Campus Sexual Misconduct," and were described as a "significant rules document." It included a statement that at some unspecified point in the future, the DOE would "engage in rulemaking on the topic of schools' Title IX responsibilities concerning complaints of sexual misconduct, including peer-on-peer sexual harassment and sexual violence. The Department will solicit input from stakeholders and the public during that rulemaking process." The document provided further that it would serve as "interim information about how the Office for Civil Rights (OCR) will assess a school's compliance with Title IX." (DeVos rules, p. 1).

The DeVos rules stated that they did not constitute new laws and were intended to replace the 2011 Dear Colleague Letter (DCL),[21] and Department of Education Guidance from 2014. (DeVos rules, p. 7). In fact, the DeVos rules rescinded or subverted state and federal laws, including Title IX and mandatory provisions of the Title IX regulations, duly promulgated in 1975, 34 C.F.R. part 106, et seq. Among other things, the DeVos rules subject sex-based harms to different and worse treatment compared to other types of civil rights harms; require the use of more onerous criminal law definitions, rather than civil rights definitions, to determine whether a sex-based civil rights offense occurred (DeVos rules, p. 2); permit application of a more onerous "clear and convincing evidence" standard of proof, rather than the civil rights standard of "preponderance of the evidence" (DeVos rules, p. 5) to determine whether a sex-based civil rights offense occurred; require schools to afford offenders of sex-based civil rights harms the same rights as victims of sex-based civil rights harms; and incorporate by reference, a 2013 amendment to the Clery Act, known popularly as the Campus SaVE Act, which permits or requires schools to apply different and worse legal standards when responding to and redressing sex-based civil rights harms.[22] The DeVos were not made applicable to harms based on other protected class categories, such as race and national origin.

Alongside less protective standards, the DeVos rules were silent on the need for schools to comply with civil rights laws at all. Indeed, the entire DeVos rules mention the phrase "civil rights" only when citing the title of the "Office For Civil Rights."

---

five stalking victims are women. By comparison, 94% of the stalkers identified by female victims and 60% of the stalkers identified by male victims were male. Overall, 87% of the stalkers identified by the victims were male. National Institute of Justice 1998. *Stalking in America: Findings from the National Violence Against Women Survey*.

[21] U.S. Dept. of Education Office for Civil Rights, Dear Colleague Letter (Apr 4, 2011), *available at* http://www2.ed.gov/about/offices/list/ocr/letters/colleague-201104.html.

[22] The Campus SaVE Act is also known as the 2013 Violence Against Women Reauthorization Act's amendments to the Clery Act. SaVE's discriminatory regulations can be found at 34 C.F.R. 668.46. See also, note 33.

The Plaintiffs

Three women and a national women's rights organization served as Plaintiffs in the Boston lawsuit. Equal Means Equal (EME), a national non-profit women's rights organization, served as a representational Plaintiff on behalf of women as a class. EME advocates for sex/gender equality, enactment of the Equal Rights Amendment, and fully equal rights for women.[23]

Plaintiff Jane Doe joined in the suit because she was involved as a complainant in an ongoing OCR investigation against Stonehill College in Massachusetts, arising out of allegations that Stonehill violated Title IX in the way that it responded to her report of sexual victimization by a Stonehill athlete. The OCR official responsible for her case declined to ensure Doe that the DeVos rules would not be applied to her case.

Plaintiff Mary Doe joined in the suit because she was involved as a plaintiff in a Massachusetts civil lawsuit against Boston University, which suit involved allegations that the university unlawfully failed to enforce her rights under Title IX, as well as the Massachusetts Constitution and state civil rights laws, after she was sexually victimized on Boston University's campus. Plaintiff Mary Doe was concerned that the DeVos rules would be used by Boston University to undermine her rights in the civil suit because lawyers for schools were already using the DeVos rules to gain an advantage against the rights of victims in other lawsuits.[24]

Plaintiff Susan Doe joined in the lawsuit because she was involved as a complainant in an ongoing OCR investigation against the School of the Art Institute of Chicago (SAIC), arising out of allegations that Doe had been severely sexually abused and exploited by her direct advisor at SAIC. The OCR official handling her case declined to assure Doe that the DeVos rules would not be applied to her case.

The Title IX Regulations

The Title IX regulations, like the statute, forbid discrimination based on sex, and state that a school "shall not, on the basis of sex," inter alia, "treat one person differently from another in determining whether such person satisfies any requirement of condition for the provision of such aid, benefit, or service; provide different aid, benefits, or services in a different manner; deny any person such aid, benefit, or service". 34 C.F.R. part 106.31(b)(1-7).

The Title IX regulations also state that a school shall not on the basis of sex "subject any person to separate or different rules of behavior, sanctions, or other

[23] https://www.equalmeansequal.org.

[24] *Kollaritsch v. Michigan State University Board of Trustees, et al.*, 1:15-cv-01191-PLM-PJG, United States District Court, Western District of Michigan (court order issued 10/17/17 denying motion to strike and granting defendants leave to file supplemental authority regarding "Significant Change in Guidance on Title IX.")

treatment, or otherwise limit any person in the enjoyment or any right, privilege, advantage or opportunity." 34 C.F.R. part 106.31(b)(1-7), and that a school "shall adopt and publish grievance procedures providing for prompt and equitable resolution of student and employee complaints alleging any action, which would be prohibited by Title IX. 34 C.F.R. part 106.8(b)." Equitable redress is also mandatory under Title IV[25] and Title VI.[26]

The Title IX regulations further state that, "A school shall implement specific and continuing steps to notify students and employees that it does not discriminate on the basis of sex," that it is "required by Title IX not to discriminate in such a manner," and that "such notification shall state that the requirement not to discriminate extends to employment..." 34 C.F.R. part 106.9(a). The Title IX regulations also forbid a school to "use or distribute a publication, which suggests by text or illustration that such school treats applicants, students or employees differently on the basis of sex." 34 C.F.R. part 106.9(b)(2).

Legal Claims Alleged in the Boston Lawsuit

The Plaintiffs alleged various claims, including that the DeVos rules violated Title IX and the Administrative Procedures Act, and that aspects of the DeVos guidance were unconstitutional to the extent they emanated from the Clery Act or the

[25] Among the University of Montana—Missoula, the U.S. Department of Justice, Civil Rights Division, Educational Opportunities Section and the U.S. Department of Education, Office for Civil Rights, RESOLUTION AGREEMENT, available at http://www.justice.gov/crt/about/edu/documents/montanaagree.pdf (announcing resolution agreement with the University of Montana and noting that Title IV and Title IX both require "equity" and are subject to the same regulations and standards of enforcement regarding discrimination, harassment, and violence in education).

[26] *Title VI Enforcement Highlights Office for Civil Rights*, U.S. DEPARTMENT OF EDUCATION (last visited Jan 30, 2014) http://www2.ed.gov/documents/press-releases/title-vi-enforcement.pdf (repeatedly noting that Title VI requires schools to apply standard of "equity"); *Title IX Legal Manual*, THE UNITED STATES DEPARTMENT OF JUSTICE (last visited Jan 30, 2014); http://www.justice.gov/crt/about/cor/coord/ixlegal.php (noting that "Congress consciously modeled Title IX on Title VI" and citing Alexander v. Choate, 469 U.S. 287, 294 (1985) (for the proposition that because Title IX and Title VI contain parallel language, thus the same analytic framework should apply because both statutes were enacted to prevent unlawful discrimination and to provide remedies for the effects of past discrimination); See also 42 U.S.C. § 2000d-7 (requiring equal treatment on behalf of all protected class categories). In a section labeled "Civil rights remedies equalization," the statute provides that "(1) A State shall not be immune under the Eleventh Amendment of the Constitution of the United States from suit in Federal court for a violation of § 504 of the Rehabilitation Act of 1973 [29 U.S.C. 794], Title IX of the Education Amendments of 1972 [20 U.S.C. 1681 et seq.], the Age Discrimination Act of 1975 [42 U.S.C. 6101 et seq.], Title VI of the Civil Rights Act of 1964 [42 U.S.C. 2000d et seq.], or the provisions of any other Federal statute prohibiting discrimination by recipients of Federal financial assistance." This "Civil rights remedies equalization" mandate further states that "(2) In a suit against a State for a violation of a statute referred to in paragraph (1), remedies (including remedies both at law and in equity) are available for such a violation ***to the same extent*** as such remedies are available for such a violation in the suit against any public or private entity other than a State." (emphasis added).

Commerce Clause because Congress has no general authority to regulate violence against women.[27] To the extent Congress has authority to regulate civil rights matters under the Spending Clause, it cannot do so in a manner that intrudes unconstitutionally into the authority of the states,[28] which the DeVos rules did because they violated Massachusetts state constitutional and civil rights laws, which grant women equality and fully equal treatment under the law.[29] The lawsuit did not seek money damages. It was a claim for declaratory and injunctive relief only, meaning the Plaintiffs were asking the court to prevent schools (and courts and agencies) from applying the DeVos rules, and to have the rules declared unlawful.

Why the DeVos Rules Violate Title IX

The DeVos rules violate Title IX for many reasons, including that they require or permit schools to treat civil rights harms differently on the basis of sex, in violation of 34 C.F.R. part 106.31(a).

The DeVos rules state that schools "should" use onerous criminal law definitions and standards, such as "sexual assault,"[30] rather than civil rights definitions of "unwelcome and offensive"[31] to determine whether sex-based civil rights harms occurred.[32] Indeed, the word "unwelcome" appears nowhere in the DeVos rules, but the criminal law term "sexual assault" appears nine times.

---

[27] *U.S. v. Morrison*, 529 U.S. 598 (2000); (Congress has no authority to regulate violence against women under civil rights laws or the Commerce Clause).

[28] *N'tl Federation of Independent Business v. Sebelius*, 567 U.S. 519 (2012) (Congress exceeds its authority under the Spending Clause if it imposes too heavy a burden on the states as a quid pro quo for receiving federal funds.

[29] See infra, pp. 15–16.

[30] The DeVos rules cites to 34 C.F.R. § 106.8(b) as support for the use of criminal law terms to describe harms addressed on campus under Title IX grievance procedures, yet those regulations were promulgated under a 2013 amendment to the Clery Act; they were not promulgated under Title IX, and at least one federal court has already ruled that those regulations can have "no effect" on Title IX because Congress cannot lawfully amend Title IX by amending the Clery Act. *Doe v. U.S. Dept. of Health and Human Services*, 85 F. Supp. 3d 1, 11 (D.D.C. 2015)

[31] "Unwelcome" is defined as conduct the student "did not request or invite it and considered the conduct to be undesirable or offensive. The age of the student, the nature of the conduct, and other relevant factors affect whether a student was capable of welcoming the sexual conduct. A student's submission to the conduct or failure to complain does not always mean that the conduct was welcome." http://www2.ed.gov/about/offices/list/ocr/docs/ocrshpam.html.

[32] This aspect of the DeVos rules also violates existing OCR guidance, issued in the form of a Dear Colleague Letter from 2010 that was not rescinded in the DeVos rules, hence remains relevant and applicable. See *Letter from Russlynn Ali*, Assistant Secretary for Civil Rights, Department of Education, Office for Civil Rights (October 26, 2010) ("The label used to describe an incident (e.g., sexual assault, bullying, hazing, teasing) does not determine how a school is obligated to respond. Rather, the nature of the conduct itself must be assessed for civil rights implications. So, for example, if the abusive behavior is on the basis of race, color, national origin, sex, or disability, and creates a hostile environment, a school is obligated to respond in accordance with the appli-

The DeVos rules also permit the use of a burden of proof more onerous than preponderance of the evidence to determine whether a sex-based civil rights harm has been proved. Secretary DeVos has stated that the Obama administration's 2011 DCL improperly changed the law to require use of the preponderance standard, and that the DeVos rules merely restored the law to permit the use of a more onerous standard by rescinding the DCL. But application of the preponderance standard was required under civil rights laws long before the DCL was released.[33] The DCL merely reminded schools of their obligation to provide "equitable" redress by applying the preponderance standard to sex-based harms, as they were doing with other civil rights matters.[34]

Applying a more onerous burden of proof only to sex-based civil rights harms obviously subjects victims of such harms to different treatment because it means that if a student were physically beaten on the basis of national origin, the matter would be resolved under a "preponderance of the evidence" standard, and if the evidence showed the offense more likely than not occurred, the offender would suffer consequences. However, if the ***exact*** same offender committed ***exactly*** the same conduct against a student on the basis of her sex, and ***exactly*** the same quality of evidence were presented, school officials could assess the evidence under the more onerous standard of clear and convincing evidence, and the offender would suffer

---

cable federal civil rights statutes and regulations enforced by OCR."); *Education & Title IX*, National Women's Law Center (last visited Jan 29, 2014), http://www.nwlc.org/our-issues/education-%2526-title-ix.

[33] Letter from Sheralyn Goldbecker, OCR D.C. Office, to John J. DeGioia, President, Georgetown University (May 5, 2004) ("[C]omplaints of sexual harassment were resolved using a clear and convincing evidence standard, a higher standard than the preponderance of the evidence standard, which is the appropriate standard under Title IX for sex discrimination complaints, including those alleging sexual harassment."); Letter from Gary D. Jackson, Regional Civil Rights Director, OCR Region X, to Jane Jervis, President, Evergreen State College (April 4, 1995) (stating that the "evidentiary standard of proof applied to Title IX actions is that of a 'preponderance of the evidence'" and that requiring 'clear and convincing proof' imposes "a heavier burden of proof than that which is required under Title IX."); OCR also uses a preponderance of the evidence standard when it resolves complaints against recipients, and in fund termination hearings. "Grievance procedures that use [a] higher standard are inconsistent with the standard of proof established for violations of the civil rights laws, and are thus *not equitable* under Title IX." See April 4, 2011 Dear Colleague Letter, p. 12. (emphasis added).

[34] That Title IX's mandate of equitable treatment requires application of the preponderance standard was acknowledged during congressional hearings related to the enactment of the Campus SaVE Act, which was a 2013 amendment of the Clery Act. One Congressman was strikingly candid about why removing the word "equitable" from the Campus SaVE Act would allow schools to apply a more onerous burden of proof on victims of sex-based harms: "The majority bill said that college campuses must provide for 'prompt and equitable investigation and resolution' of charges of violence or stalking. This would have codified a proposed rule of the Department of Education that would have required imposition of a civil standard or preponderance of the evidence for what is essentially a criminal charge, one that, if proved, rightly should harm reputation. But if established on a barely "more probable than not" standard, reputations can be ruined unfairly and very quickly. The substitute eliminates this provision." (Testimony of Senator Grassley, Iowa, 158 Cong Rec. S 2761, Congressional Record, Sen., 112th Congress, 2nd Session Senate, April 26, 2012; Violence Against Women Reauthorization Act of 2011, Reference: Vol. 158, No. 61).

no consequences. Applying a more onerous burden of proof only in sex-based matters would also mean that the redress of certain claims would be subject to absurd dual assessments. For example, if a black woman were assaulted on the basis of her race ***and*** her sex at a school that opted to apply the "clear and convincing evidence" standard, that single civil rights offense would be subjected to two different burdens of proof. Even more strangely, because the DeVos rules cover only the most serious and severe forms of sex-based civil rights harms, a student who endures less serious verbal harassment would continue to have her civil rights redressed under the preponderance standard. This means that offenders of the most serious forms of sex-based civil rights infractions would be less likely to be held responsible compared to less serious verbal offenders.

Finally, the DeVos rules require schools to incorporate the standards, terms, definitions, and procedures set forth in the Campus SaVE Act, (DeVos rules, p. 2), which violates Title IX's prohibition on different treatment because, like the DeVos rules, the SaVE Act permits or requires the use of more onerous standards and definitions than those required by civil rights laws.[35]

In addition to Title IX's general prohibition against different treatment based on sex, the DeVos rules violate particular provisions of the Title IX regulations, including those that forbid different treatment with regard to "rules of behavior, sanctions, or other treatment." 34 C.F.R. part 106.31(b)(1-7), and "aids, benefits and/or services," 34 C.F.R. part 106.31(b)(1-7). The DeVos rules also allow schools to use or distribute a publication, "which suggests by text or illustration that such school treats applicants, students or employees differently on the basis of sex," in violation of 34 C.F.R. part 106.9(b)(2).

Because the DeVos rules unlawfully subject victims of sex-based harms to separate and different treatment, particularly regarding the use of more onerous criminal law definitions rather than civil rights definitions, and application of a burden of proof more onerous than preponderance, to determine whether a sex-based civil rights offense occurred, they necessarily limit such victims "in the enjoyment of their rights, privileges, advantages and opportunities," in violation of 34 C.F.R. part 106.31(b)(1-7). For similar reasons, the DeVos rules prevent "prompt and equitable" redress in the resolution of "student and employee complaints alleging any action, which would be prohibited by Title IX," in violation of 34 C.F.R. part 106.8(b).

[35] Supra, notes 21 and 33.

Why the DeVos Rules Violate the Administrative Procedures Act

The Administrative Procedures Act (APA) mandates that agencies promulgate new rules only within certain substantive limitations, and only after certain procedural rules have been followed. Substantive limitations and procedural rules include that an agency may not issue rules in excess of statutory jurisdiction, authority, or limitations, or short of statutory right; or that are contrary to constitutional right, power, privilege, or immunity. Nor may such rules be arbitrary and capricious, an abuse of discretion, or otherwise not in accordance with law. Finally, subject to narrow exceptions, new rules may not be issued until after a notice and comment period, which gives the public an opportunity to review proposed rules, changes and provide feedback prior to issuance.

The Boston lawsuit alleged numerous violations of the APA, including that Secretary DeVos acted outside her jurisdiction and authority because an agency can only promulgate rules and regulations in furtherance of a statute; it cannot subvert a statute by issuing rules that subject victims of sex-based harms to different and worse treatment when the statute itself forbids sex discrimination. In addition, the lawsuit alleged that because the DeVos rules subjected sex-based harms to different and worse treatment, they violated the APA because they were contrary to constitutional right, were arbitrary and capricious, and not in accordance with law. Finally, the lawsuit alleged that the DeVos rules violated the APA because they were issued before the public was given notice and a chance to comment.

Why the DeVos Rules Violate the First Amendment

The lawsuit included a claim that the DeVos rules violate the First Amendment because by subjecting victims of sex-based harm to different and worse treatment on campus, victims would be less willing to report sex-based harms, or seek redress on campus, for fear their rights under Title IX would not fully be enforced.[36] The First Amendment permits preemptive legal proceedings, before an individual suffers a violation of rights from the application of the DeVos rules in an actual case, on the grounds that if persons are inhibited from reporting civil rights harms and seeking redress, a "chilling effect" occurs, which is sufficient legal injury to justify the filing of a lawsuit.[37]

---

[36] Supra note 2, quoting the National Women's Law Center and Senator Bob Casey (D. PA.) saying the new DeVos rules will discourage victims from coming forward.

[37] *Waters v. Churchill*, 511 U.S. 661, 669 (1994) (where First Amendment rights are threatened, courts relax the prudential requirement of actual injury in light of the weightier concern of the chilling effect on free speech).

Why the DeVos Rules Violate Massachusetts Law

The lawsuit was filed in Massachusetts, thus implicating Massachusetts state civil rights and constitutional rights laws. Massachusetts General Law, Chapter 93, § 102, the Massachusetts Equal Rights Act, guarantees females the full and equal benefit of all laws and proceedings for the security of persons …" The lawsuit alleged that the DeVos rules violated the Massachusetts Equal Rights Act by denying females the full and equal benefit of laws and proceedings for the security of their persons. The suit also asserted that, for similar reasons, the DeVos rules violated the Equal Protection Clause of Part 1, Article I of the Massachusetts Constitution, which prohibits discriminatory and unequal treatment based on sex. Unlike claims of sex discrimination under the federal constitution, claims of sex/gender discrimination under the Massachusetts Constitution are subject to strict scrutiny.[38]

What's Next?

No doubt when the DOE undertakes to codify the DeVos rules by amending the Title IX regulations during the notice and rulemaking process, they will remove all provisions from the existing regulations that currently prohibit "separate" and "different" treatment based on sex. While this will ostensibly permit schools to subject victims of sex-based harms to different and worse treatment, including use of criminal law definitions and application of the clear and convincing evidence standard, lawsuits like the one filed in Boston will continue to be filed in federal courts around the country on the grounds that regulations promulgated under a specific statute must advance, not subvert, that statute's purpose. Thus, the argument will go, it is unlawful for a federal agency to use its delegated authority to promulgate regulations that permit unequal treatment as this would undermine the Title IX statute's prohibition against discrimination based on sex. Only Congress can change a statute; the DOE cannot.

It may well come to be that Congress, like the DOE, will take steps to weaken Title IX because several bills have been proposed which, if enacted, will weaken Title IX at its core. The Campus Accountability and Safety Act (CASA) is one such bill. Other laws proposed at the federal level promise to protect Title IX, but will weaken Title IX instead, including a bill filed by Congresswoman Jackie Speier. Both proposals will allow schools to subject civil rights violence against women to separate, different, and worse rules, compared to civil rights violence based on other protected class categories, such as race and national origin.

At the state level, harmful laws that permit separate, different, and worse treatment include New York's already enacted "enough is enough" law. A similar law has been proposed in California and other states. Even the American Bar Association's

[38] *Commonwealth v. King*, 374 Mass. 5, 21 (1977).

(ABA) is supporting the unequal treatment of women in a strange new policy on Title IX that urges schools to subject only sex-based harms to separate, different, and worse treatment compared to civil rights harms based on other protected class categories, such as race and national origin. The ABA reportedly adopted its formal policy in 2017 so that it could lobby for new federal and state laws to weaken women's civil rights.

Advocates who care about women's equality should be mobilizing politically against these efforts, and should aggressively be demanding that people leave Title IX (and state law analogues) alone. Title IX is perfect the way it is because it mandates equal treatment, and forbids discrimination based on sex. Women need better enforcement of their civil rights, not new laws. Equality in education is what they fought for and won nearly 50 years ago. Equality is what they have now, and equality is what they deserve.

Women in Leadership

Sharlyn Moore and Andrea Diese

Don't just stand for the success of other women—insist on it.

Gail Blanke

Some are surprised at what little has changed since the 1960s, and 1970s when considering women's role in the workplace. However, some remarkable cultural shifts have occurred, many are positive in supporting the evolution of women's work and standing in organizations. Regarding the empirical data, the Census Bureau reports that women employed in the workforce have increased from 30.3 million in 1970 to 72.7 million during 2006–2010. Today, women make up almost 50% of the workforce; in addition, women have made significant gains in certain occupations that were male dominated, such as accountants, police officers, lawyers, judges, physicians, surgeons, and pharmacists (Baig, 2013).

With all the strong positive movement for women in the workforce, some things have not changed, and the Mad Men era is still alive and well. Women still dominate as dental assistants, administrative assistants (which has been upgraded from the title of secretaries), registered nurses, and elementary school teachers. The leading occupations for women in the 1970s are still the prominent professions for women today. The conversations will continue to occur regarding issues that women face in the workforce; however, it is shocking that the same conversations today are what we were talking about in the 1960s and 1970s. It is time to move forward, evolve as a society, and continue to improve the American organizational culture by infusing a focus on equality.

S. Moore
Sterling Marketing Management & Consulting, Stephens City, VA, USA
e-mail: Sharlyn@sterlingmmc.com

A. Diese (✉)
American College of Commerce and Technology, Falls Church, VA, USA
e-mail: andrea.diese@acct.edu

F. L. Denmark, M. A. Paludi (eds.), *Women and Leadership*,
https://doi.org/10.1007/978-3-319-72182-8_8

All Things Being Equal: Does Gender Still Matter?

Women won the right to vote on August 18, 1902, with the ratification of the 19th Amendment. Amelia Earhart was the first woman aviator to fly alone across the Atlantic Ocean, and Shirley Chisholm was the first black woman elected to U.S. Congress. Women are more educated than ever before and arguably have been more visibly successful in the workforce. One may arrive at the assumption that with such strides in the advancements in humanity, something as fundamental as the concept of equality between men and women within the workplace would no longer need to be discussed. The question is, does gender matter?

In truth, in 2017 men and women are still not considered equal in the workplace. According to a study entitled Women in the Workplace 2016 by LeanIn.org, the glass ceiling still exists, and the disparaging difference in pay between men and women is not only significant, but the number of women that achieve the c-suite is not comparable. View Fig. 1. This study entailed an assessment of 132 global companies. The information obtained from this study was used to provide information to key leadership regarding the efforts they could take to help promote and put into practical application practices that support a more inclusive environment. More than 34,000 employees participated in the survey that touched upon areas including but not limited to pay, promotion, the perception of job satisfaction, and work/life balance matters.

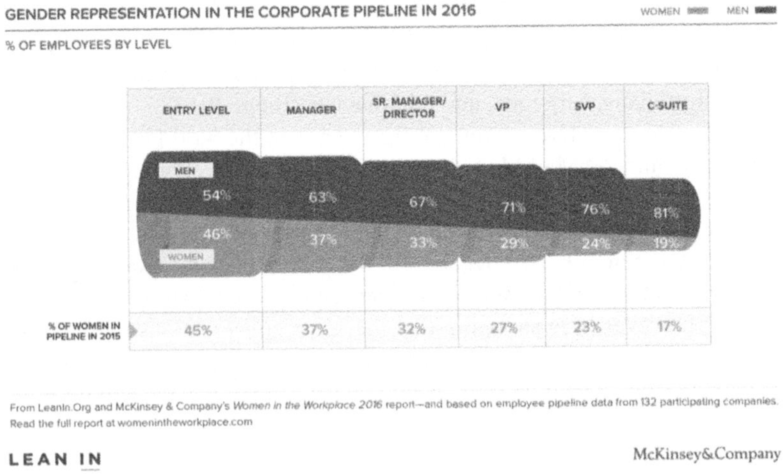

From the graph, the data demonstrates that with the higher rank in position, the lower the number of women that hold that senior level position decreases significantly. Have women not sufficiently demonstrated that they are equally capable of performing said tasks or requirements?

According to Zenger and Folkman (2012), women are consistently rated higher than men in leadership competencies such as taking initiative, practicing self-development, displaying higher integrity and honesty, drive for results, developing others, inspiring and motivating others, and building relationships. The data shows that we have more women in the workplace than any decade before; however, these exemplary women leaders are not commanding the top executive positions. Is it deliberate discrimination because the leadership abilities of their counterparts intimidate men? With all the research provided, the question remains, what can women do?

Strategies

The reason that women believe they rate higher than men in leadership qualities such as taking the initiative and practicing self-development is because they must work twice as hard to prove themselves to the top leaders of an organization. Both women and top leaders of an organization must contribute to strategically changing the culture and bias of women in the workforce. A leader must look for the top talent, no matter what the gender, and demand the best. Women have already proven that they can take on the challenge and will accept the position with the determination to take the initiative, perform with integrity and set the example to inspire others.

Women still have some work to do, even though they already feel the pressure to demonstrate their talent and worth. Considering that women outperform men when it comes to building relationships, they need to use that skill to network. Networking events should be a priority to continue the growth for advancement and obtain a position in an industry that is male dominated or accepting a top-level executive status.

Some believe that there is a finite number of positions available for women, this is just not the case. The truth is, there are plenty of positions of power, and success is not a limited resource. We need to change our perspective and understand that there is a copious number of jobs for all, women breaking the glass ceiling does not mean it is at the expense of men. Over time, the perception will shift to an understanding that the truly talented leader was awarded the position.

Keep in mind, as was stated above, there is an abundance of positions in the workplace; therefore, women need to aim higher. Dream big, do the proper research and do not settle for a modest goal or salary. Women should shift their beliefs and know they are empowered to achieve whatever they aspire to be in the workplace. The following are some other key strategies that women should consider as they contemplate their career growth.

Perform an Assessment

If you do not have a plan, plan to fail. It is imperative for you to assess your department or group and ultimately that of the organization. You need to understand the lay of the land. Without performing a fundamental organizational analysis, you may miss identifying critical and essential aspects that influence the culture and ultimate power structure of the organization.

Collaboration (Make Them Think that It's Their Idea)

Creating buy-in within a group, cohort, or organization is not a new concept. Any leader worth his or her salt understands the importance of the fundamental application of buy-in. As a leader, it is your responsibility to steer the ship. However, being a jack of all trades and a master of none serves no one. There is no question that women face the conundrum of perception. Meaning, a woman states XYZ and may be considered aggressive. A man reports XYZ and he is merely expressing his opinion. Is this perspective perception or reality? The proof, as they say, is in the pudding.

Stop Saying Sorry/Apologizing (Be a Politician)

It seems almost second nature for women to apologize for the most minute thing. Is it possible that doing so places women in more of a subservient role? Turn on any media or news outlet, and you will see a politician espousing his or her values to whoever would listen. If you observe carefully, you will be hard pressed to find one that overtly says sorry. In the eyes of the public, doing so is an admission of guilt. There are other ways to acknowledge a mistake without saying the actual words. "I do not recall that event." The question then becomes, are we really sorry or is it something we say to placate ourselves as much as the other potentially offended party?

Sheryl Sandberg, who is the Chief Operating Officer of Facebook, noted that one day while giving a talk, she was performing the question and answers portion. She informed the group that she would only answer one more question. The women in the group stopped raising their hands, and the men continued to raise their hands and had their questions answered. One of the young ladies approached Ms. Sandberg and informed her of what she had observed. Ms. Sandberg apologized. The young lady said that she learned not to stop raising her hand.

Emotional Intelligence: Don't Leave Home Without It

Emotional intelligence is the one thing that you should keep in your daily arsenal, for better or for worse. Emotional intelligence is systematically one of the most underutilized tools in the workplace and within the leadership arena. With so much information being readily available, we must ask ourselves why? Should we postulate that it is a lack of the knowledge of the concept or does the trouble lie in moving from the subjective to reality as it relates to its practical application? Many understand that there are those who have a certain degree of vanity and appreciate a modicum of praise. We have seen repeatedly how personal ambition and hubris can and will drive an organization in a direction that is not beneficial to the organization's well-being; Enron, WorldCom, Bear Sterns, and Time Warner, to name a few.

Understand that there are external forces at work that need to be considered. With the consistent inclusion of technology into our lives, the need for constant contact, stimulation, and to show people how important we are, narcissism is part of our daily interactions whether we like it or not. So why use emotional intelligence? How does it help me? Emotional intelligence is your ace up your sleeve. It should be known in leadership 101 that it is not about what the leader wants, it is about what the people need.

References

Baig, M., (2013). Women in the workforce: What changes have we made? *The Huffington Post*. Retrieved from https://www.huffingtonpost.com/mehroz-baig/women-in-the-workforce-wh_b_4462455.html.

Zenger, J., & Folkman, J. (2012). Are women better leaders than men? *Harvard Business Review*. Retrieved from https://hbr.org/2012/03/a-study-in-leadership-women-do.

Appendix

Organizations Concerned with Women and Leadership

Michele A. Paludi Savannah White
Excelsior College
Albany, NY, USA
mpaludi@excelsior.edu

Advancing Women in Leadership

www.advancingwomen.com/awl/awl.html
African American Women's Leadership
http://www.ncnw.org
Alliance of Women Entrepreneurs
http://www.awe-westmichigan.org/
American Business Women's Association (ABWA)
http://www.abwa.org/pages/home-page
Association for Women in Communications
http://www.womcom.org/
Athena Center for Leadership Studies
https://athenacenter.barnard.edu/
Athena Foundation
http://www.athenafoundation.org/
Black Women's Leadership Council
http://www.bwlc.com/
The Boston Club
http://www.thebostonclub.com/
Business and Professional Women's Foundation
http://www.bpwfoundation
Caribbean Institute for Women and Leadership

F. L. Denmark, M. A. Paludi (eds.), *Women and Leadership*,
https://doi.org/10.1007/978-3-319-72182-8

http://caribbean.unwomen.org/en/news-and-events/events/2011/7/the-caribbean-institute-for-women-in-leadership---ciwil
Catalyst
http://www.catalyst.org/
Center for Creative Leadership
http://www.ccl.org
Center for Leadership and Change Management
http://www.leadership.wharton.upenn.edu
Center for Asian Pacific American Women
http://www.apawomen.org
Center for Women's Business Research
http://womensbusinessresearch.org/
Center for Women's Global Leadership
http://www.cwgl.rutgers.edu
Center for Women's Intercultural Leadership
http://www.centerforwomeninleadership.org/#/
Center for Women's Leadership, Babson College
http://www.babon.edu/cwl
Chattanooga Women's Leadership Institute
http://www.cwli.org/index.php
Community of Women Entrepreneurs
http://www.reformsnetwork.org/women/
Council of Women World Leaders
http://www.womenworldleaders.org
Courageous Leadership Consortium
http://www.courageousleadership.org
eWomen Network
https://www.ewomennetwork.com/
Ellevate Network
https://www.ellevatenetwork.com/
Executive Women International
http://www.executive women.org/
Foundation for Women's Resources
http://womensresources.org/LT.asp
Global Exec Women
http://www.globalexecwomen.com
Global Women's Leadership Initiative
https://www.wilsoncenter.org/program/global-womens-leadership-initiative
Harpswell Foundation Leadership Centers for Women
http://www.harpswellfoundation.org
IGNITE
http://www.ignitenational.org/our_story
Institute for Women's Leadership
http://www.womensleadership.com
International Women's Democracy Center

https://iwdc.org/
Invent Your Future Enterprises
http://inventourfuture.com
James MacGregor Burns Academy of Leadership
http://www.academy.umd.edu/home/
Leadership America
http://www.leadershipamaerica.com
Leadership California
http://www.leadershipca.org
Leadership Institute
https://www.stkate.edu/academics/institutes-and-centers/
Leadership Illinois
http://leadershipillinois.org
Leadership Texas
http://www.womensresources.org/LT.asp
National African American Women's Leadership Institute, Inc.
http://www.naawli.org
National Association for Female Executives
http://nafe.com
National Association of Professional Women (NAPW)
https://www.napw.com/
National Association of Women Business Owners
http://nawbo.org
National Association of Women MBA's
http://nawmba.org/?
National Council of Women's Organizations
http://www.womensorganizations.org/
National Hispana Leadership Institute
http://www.nhli.org
National Latina Business Women Association (NLBWA)
http://www.nlbwa.org/
National Organization for Women
http://www.now.org/
National Women's Business Council (NWBC)
https://www.nwbc.gov/
NYU Women's Leadership Forum
http://www.nyu.edu/students/communities-and-groups/student-diversity.html
Organization of Women Leaders
http://owls.wordpress.com/
Rutgers University Center for Women and Politics
http://www.cawp.rutgers.edu/education_training/trainingresources/index.php
She Should Run
http://www.sheshouldrun.org/mission
Seattle Women's Commission
http://www.seattle.gov/womenscommission/resources.htm

Soroptimist International
http://www.soroptimist.org
South Asian Women's Leadership Forum
http://www.southasianwomen.org/
Susan B. Anthony Center for Women's Leadership
http://www.rochester.edu./sba/rsources.html
The Coaching and Mentoring Network
http://www.coachingnetwork.org.uk
Virginia Women's Institute for Leadership
http://www.mbc.edu/vwil/
Vital Voices
https://www.vitalvoices.org/
Women's Business Exchange
http://www.wbex.org/
Women Entrepreneur
http://www.womenentrepreneur.com/interstitial/default.com/
Women Executive Leadership
http://www.womenexecutiveleadership.com/
Women's Executive Network
http://www.wxnetwork.com
Women's Leadership Academy
http://www.albany.edu/womeningov/programs/wli.shtml
Women's Leadership Conference
https://womensleadershipconference.gwu.edu/
Women in Leadership Foundation
http://www.womeninleadership.ca/
Women's Leadership Initiative
https://admissions.yale.edu/womens-leadership-initiative
Women Leaders Online
http://www.wlo.org
Women's Foundation of California
http://www.womensfoundca.orgsite/c.aqKGLROAIrH/B.963905/k.FA88/Womens_Found
Women's Institute for Leadership Development for Human Rights
http://www.wildforhumanrights.org
Women's Leadership Circles
http://www.w-l-c.org/content/print.php
Women's Leadership Exchange
http://www.womensleadershipexchange.com/
Women's Leadership Forum
http://www.exed.hbs.edu/programs/wlf/
Women's Leadership Institute
http://www.mills.edu/WLI/wli.home.html
Women's Leadership Network
http://wlnhelena.org/

Women's Leadership Program
http://www.ccl.org/leadership/programs/WLPOverview.aspx
Women's Learning Partnership
http://www.learningpartnership.org/
Women of Color Leadership Institute
http://www.nmac.org/index/wocli
Women in Law Leadership
http://www.abanet.org/women/will.html
Women Presidents Organization
http://www.wprog.com/index.htm
World Association for Women Entrepreneurs
http://www.fcem.org/www/default/asp
Worldwide Guide to Women in Leadership
http://www.guide2womenleaders.com
Women Unlimited, Inc.
https://www.women-unlimited.com/about-us/
WomenWatch
http://www.un.org/womenwatch
Young Female Entrepreneurs
http://youngfemaleentrepreneurs.com/
ZONTA International
https://www.zonta.org/

Index

F. L. Denmark, M. A. Paludi (eds.), *Women and Leadership*,
https://doi.org/10.1007/978-3-319-72182-8